Praise For

If I Tell You I'm Gay, Will You Still Love Me?

While the culture may celebrate the coming out of so many men and women, Christian parents are often devastated and confused when a son or daughter announces "I'm gay." They need to hear from someone who's been there, and Ann Mobley's book provides them a comforting shoulder to weep on and some godly wisdom to rely on. I especially appreciate her tone, and her vulnerability, in putting this hugely needed work together. It couldn't be timelier.

Joe Dallas, Author of
When Homosexuality Hits Home and *The Game Plan*

I would strongly encourage every pastor—indeed every staff member, teacher, ministry leader, youth worker and certainly every parent—to keep this book on their desk. It is very readable, drawing you in from the first page. It maintains a level of interest throughout and contains a wealth of extremely valuable information and insight for dealing not only with this very complex subject, but with those who are impacted by it. Get this book. Get several copies of this book so you will have it available when someone you know needs it—and sooner or later that will happen.

Bob Stith, Former National Strategist for Gender Issues
The Southern Baptist Convention

Ann Mobley is truly a woman of grace and knowledge. She embodies and conveys both the biblical wisdom and godly compassion needed to address this important topic. She combines her spiritual insight with a solid understanding of the psychological aspects of homosexuality to present an excellent resource for Christian families.

Julie Harren Hamilton, Ph.D.
Licensed Marriage and Family Therapist

It was my great joy to read Ann's book. I think the Lord will use *If I Tell You I'm Gay, Will You Still Love Me?* to encourage loved ones and give a measure of hope. It is instructive, insightful, and practical. I must not leave out compassionate. It is that as well.

Dr. Monte Shinkle, Senior Pastor
Concord Baptist Church, Jefferson City, MO

If I Tell You I'm
GAY,
Will You Still
Love Me?

One Mother's Journey to Truth and Grace

Ann Mobley

CROSSBOOKS
PUBLISHING

CrossBooks™
A Division of LifeWay
1663 Liberty Drive
Bloomington, IN 47403
www.crossbooks.com
Phone: 1-866-879-0502

All scripture quotations, unless otherwise indicated, are taken from the Holy Bible,
New International Version®, NIV®. Copyright ©1973, 1978, 1984, 2011 by Biblica, Inc.™
Used by permission of Zondervan. All rights reserved worldwide. www.zondervan.com.
The "NIV" and "New International Version" are trademarks registered in the United
States Patent and Trademark Office by Biblica, Inc.™. All rights reserved.

Scripture quotations marked "ESV" are taken from *The Holy Bible, English
Standard Version.* Copyright © 2000; 2001 by Crossway Bibles, a division
of Good News Publishers. Used by Permission. All right reserved.

Scripture quotations marked "NKJV" are taken from the New King James Version.
Copyright © 1982 by Thomas Nelson, Inc. Used by permission. All rights reserved.

Scripture quotations marked "NASB" are taken from the *New American
Standard Bible,* © Copyright 1960, 1962, 1963, 1968, 1971, 1972, 1973,
1975, 1977 by The Lockman Foundation. Used by permission.

Italics in scripture quotation indicate the author's added emphasis.

Testimonies of the four individuals in the chapter: "Change: A
Possibility? A Reality?" have been used with their permission.

The four partners of author's son are identified only by first names, and three
of those names are pseudonyms. True first name is used of one partner by
permission of his mother. Name of sexual abuser is also a pseudonym.

Biographical photo: Shirley Marsh, Spill My Cup Photography.

First published by CrossBooks 11/12/2013

ISBN: 978-1-4627-3245-6 (sc)
ISBN: 978-1-4627-3247-0 (hc)
ISBN: 978-1-4627-3246-3 (e)

Library of Congress Control Number: 2013918287

Printed in the United States of America.

To my son Dan

For his courage and willingness to allow me to
share our journey so openly and his encouragement
to write this book: "Because other parents need
to know it's okay to love their gay kid."

Table of Contents

Acknowledgments

I first want to express a special word of appreciation to Nick Harrison, an acquisitions editor who—after hearing my "Parent Testimony" at a national conference—encouraged me to consider writing this book. Without his strong, enduring belief in the need for this book and his helpful advice and unwavering support toward publication, this book wouldn't exist. Thank you, Nick!

As a first-time author, one important piece of advice I received was to have competent people read my work and give me honest feedback. I was blessed to have two very capable people fill that important role for me, each contributing unique gifts and skills. Francis Allston gave liberally of his limited time to review each chapter as I completed it and offered keen insight and honest feedback. Carol Eighmey, in addition to reviewing each chapter, offered her experienced editing skills, scrutinizing each page of the manuscript not just once, but several times to assure it was worded well and was "clean" for the first submission to the publisher. She continued to give additional time to assist me through the important final editing phases. I am deeply grateful to both these good friends for their valuable contributions.

The apostle Paul in his letters to the early church often voiced his need for their prayers. I, too, felt my own deep need for prayer support on my book journey, and a number of faithful praying friends, scattered around the country, became my Book Prayer Support Group. They never abandoned me or grew weary over the long process, but continued to lift my specific needs to the throne room of our Father. Thank you, dear friends, not only for offering up your prayers, but also for your ongoing encouragement to keep pressing forward to completion and publication of this book. You played an integral role in this book becoming a reality.

To all others who have blessed me with well-timed words or tangible support, I am deeply grateful.

In his well-known book *Experiencing God,* Dr. Henry Blackaby coined the phrase "a god-sized assignment" for a task given by God that could only be accomplished by his enabling and provision. That phrase aptly describes how I viewed writing this book.

Most importantly, my greatest acknowledgment must be to my gracious Father, who equipped me with everything good so I could do his will (Hebrews 13:21 ESV) and continued to manifest his faithfulness throughout this endeavor in so many ways. Ultimately, to him belongs all the glory and praise.

Introduction

The moral landscape of America has changed dramatically since 1992 when my son informed me of his gay identity. Homosexual advocates have made great inroads into the culture of America, moving closer to their stated goal of same-sex behavior and relationships being viewed as natural and normal and therefore accepted on an equal status, legally and socially, with opposite-sex relationships.

The myth of the undocumented "gay gene" is now firmly entrenched in the minds of most of the general public as an established fact—that same-sex orientation is sealed in concrete by nature because of genetic or biological factors and cannot be changed. Therefore, to imply in any way that homosexual behavior is unnatural and immoral is seen as intolerant, cruel, and unchristian.

In addition, there is a growing and concerted effort to indoctrinate our children and youth in the public schools that same-sex practices and relationships are normal and acceptable sexual expressions, and any opposition or variance to that view is labeled bigoted and hateful.

The escalating visibility and acceptance of homosexuality in our culture underscores a growing need to address the homosexual issue from a biblical perspective. Increasing numbers of Christian parents are hearing the troubling words from their son or daughter, "There's something I have to tell you. I'm gay," and will face the dilemma of how they should respond to their gay child. It will become more difficult for Christian parents to stand against the cultural tide of tolerance and affirmation of homosexuality while at the same time it is increasingly crucial that they stay true to the biblical position of loving the homosexual but calling homosexual behavior wrong and sinful before God.

The message of the sinfulness of homosexual conduct cannot be abandoned because, contrary to what is being preached by the homosexual community, it is actually a message of love, not hate, for the homosexual. It is good news for all sinners that God so loved the world that he gave his Son, Jesus Christ, to come to Earth to provide forgiveness and salvation from our sins. It is good news because Jesus Christ can bring change and hope to individuals trapped in sinful behaviors and enable them to be the persons God created them to be as they walk each day in a personal relationship with him.

Today and for the future, Christian parents must be informed and equipped to understand the homosexual condition while still upholding the biblical position on homosexual behavior and also demonstrating love to their gay-identified son or daughter. This same readiness is likewise needed by churches and individual Christians to enable them to respond in an informed and grace-filled way to those who struggle with same-sex attractions or are engaged in homosexual practices.

My prayer is that God will use this book to help others better understand gay people, display compassion without compromising the truth of Scripture, and love them with God's unconditional love.

Chapter 1

A Shocking Disclosure

"If we could begin to grasp, to truly understand, the depth and immeasurable magnitude of God's great love for us, we would be able to face any situation that might come into our lives." How confidently I spoke those words with deep passion and heartfelt conviction at the conclusion of the Bible study I taught at my church that Sunday morning. But I was totally unaware of how that statement would be tested in my own life that very afternoon. There was no warning—not even a whisper of apprehension—that the day would be anything but a regular Easter Sunday.

The day had begun with the eager anticipation of all that Easter Sundays typically hold: special church services filled with glorious, celebrative music and joyful greetings of "Christ is risen!" to fellow worshippers, followed by the happy response, "He is risen indeed!" I have always loved Easter Sundays, with their joyous commemoration of the resurrection of Jesus Christ and all the wonderful hope it holds for believers.

My young adult son Dan no longer attended church regularly, but on Easter he would faithfully join me for morning worship service and then come to my house for dinner afterward. Our family was now just the two of us since my husband and Dan's father, Jerry, died unexpectedly on Easter several years earlier after a brief illness, when Dan was only twelve. That loss was compounded three and a half years later when my older son Nathan was killed in a motorcycle accident.

Dan had moved out of our home at twenty-three to share an apartment with a friend—or so I thought. Now twenty-five, Dan and I had a close, loving relationship and enjoyed spending time together. I was proud of the responsible young man he had become and thankful that, as he had grown into manhood, we had not drifted apart but instead maintained a strong, emotionally healthy mother/son relationship.

I wanted our Easter dinner to be special, so I prepared the traditional ham along with other foods I knew Dan enjoyed and made his favorite dessert. After dessert and coffee, we lingered at the dining room table. During the brief silence, I was praying about how to bring up a difficult subject I wanted to discuss with him, but before I could say anything, he began speaking in a halting, trembling voice.

"Mom, there's something I have to tell you . . . I'm gay."

At first, I couldn't respond. I sat there in stunned disbelief, thinking surely Dan hadn't said what I thought I had heard.

Tears streamed down Dan's face as he continued. "I'm tired of lying to you and deceiving you. I've wanted to tell you for a long time, but I was so afraid you wouldn't love me anymore, and Mom, I couldn't handle that. You're all I've got."

I didn't realize at that moment how important my initial response to my son's confession would be. But when I saw the pain so evident on his face, I quickly moved to where he was sitting at the end of the table, put my arms around him, and drew him next to my heart. Struggling to keep my own emotions under control, I assured him, "Danny, you're my son, and I love you. Nothing is ever going to change that."

We moved to the living room where we could talk more comfortably. For Dan, a floodgate had been opened, and a torrent of words, emotions, unexpressed struggles, and confessions he had long kept stored up came pouring out. He began telling me things I wished I wasn't hearing, but as hard as it was to hear, I was glad he felt he could now be honest with me.

He explained that when he moved out of our home two years earlier, he had told me he would be sharing an apartment and expenses with a good friend, Matt. But Matt was more than a friend—he was Dan's homosexual lover. I knew he and Matt had later upgraded from the apartment to a large house with a swimming pool and three more guys had moved in with them. I had naively assumed more roommates made it possible for Dan and Matt to afford the larger home and pool. But now Dan was telling me all five of the young men were gay, and two of them were couples.

The others in the house kept urging Dan, "You have to come out to your mother. You're the only one whose parents don't know." But Dan's response had been "You don't understand the relationship I have with my mom. We're close, and I couldn't stand her turning away from me." So he continued putting off telling me.

Dan confessed he always thought he was different from other boys, and that he felt isolated as a child and teenager. He reminded me that his close friends growing up were usually girls because he felt more comfortable with them.

He pointed out interests and activities he had engaged in when he was younger, interests he considered feminine in nature and explained how, in his mind, these were more evidence he was gay. He had enjoyed creating ceramics, making and selling candles, even learning how to crochet a small throw rug, and now he was discovering he liked to cook. At that point, I interrupted him.

"Wait a minute!" I exclaimed. "Just because you like to cook is no indication you're gay. Most of the great chefs are male, not female, and what about our friend Frank? He likes to cook. In fact, he fixes dinner every night for his family. That doesn't make him gay. He's definitely a man's man. There's not a feminine bone in his body!"

"But, Mom, I'm physically attracted to guys, not girls. I have these strong, physical desires toward men." Only by God's grace was I able to respond in a calm manner to that statement.

"Son, just because you have those feelings and desires doesn't make it right to act on them. God designed sex for the marriage union between a man and a woman, and any other sexual union is wrong. Your dad and I had a good marriage, and that included a good sexual relationship. When he died, my sexual desires didn't die with him. I still had those desires, but that didn't mean I could go out and find someone to have sex with to satisfy those desires."

Dan didn't have an answer to that. I wondered later if his lack of response was because he was trying to assimilate this new thought or because he was not accustomed to thinking about his mother and father having a good sex life.

He confessed he had struggled with homosexual feelings and desires for a long time. He believed he was born gay and could not change. This was just who he was, and he had to accept it. Then Dan looked me straight in the face and exclaimed, "Mom, I love Matt! I'm happy now, and I know we're going to be together forever." I could tell he really believed that.

Dan also confirmed that afternoon what I had begun to suspect and had planned to talk to him about earlier at the dinner table. At the age of thirteen, he had been sexually molested and drawn into a sexual relationship by a trusted friend of our family. The molestation began just a few months after the death of Dan's father and had continued for most of his teenage years.

We continued to talk for several hours. Outwardly, I appeared calm and in control, but inwardly, throughout the whole conversation, I felt numb and detached. The situation seemed surreal, like I was floating somewhere up close to the ceiling, looking down on this mother and her son talking, but that mother wasn't me. It was some other mother and her son.

In contrast, Dan's whole demeanor had changed. He looked relieved, like a huge burden had been lifted off him. As he prepared to leave, we hugged and said "I love you" to each other. Then I watched him walk out the door.

Still feeling removed from the reality of what had just transpired, I proceeded to place a couple of phone calls as though this had been any other typical Sunday afternoon. I made a planned call to long-time friends in another city and carried on a normal conversation, never mentioning to them what I had just learned about my son.

Next I placed my customary Sunday afternoon call to my elderly mother in Missouri and, throughout our long conversation, never gave any indication of the devastating news I had received earlier about my son and her grandson. I could not yet wrap my mind around this unexpected development. I was still in a state of shock, disbelief, and denial.

Glancing at the clock, I suddenly realized what time it was and that I was going to be late for the Easter Cantata the choir was presenting that night at church. I quickly drove to the church, and since the program had already begun, I slipped into a back row and sat by myself. Strangely, up to this point, I had not shed any tears over the events of the day, but the first strains of familiar Easter anthems triggered the well of emotions I had so painstakingly capped that afternoon, and I could sense them persistently pushing their way up inside of me. I knew I had to get out of there before I totally lost it.

Quickly, I slipped out of the pew and into the foyer of the church, but as I pushed open the doors to the street, I discovered rain was pouring down like solid sheets of water. *How appropriate*, I thought.

The downpour matched the torrential flood of emotions threatening to engulf me. Instead of going outside, I went to the area of the building where the church offices were located so I could use the phone in my office. (I was the business administrator at the church, and thankfully, my office was not far from the sanctuary.)

I called my best friend Jan, and as soon as I heard her voice, the tears began to flow. I struggled to get words out so she could understand, and I finally managed to say, "I need to come to your house."

I went back to the exterior doors of the church and stepped out into the pouring rain. Water was rushing down the street, cresting at the top of the curb. I took off my shoes and waded across the street to the parking lot and my car. By the time I climbed into the car, I was drenched, but it didn't matter.

The sheets of rain slamming against the windshield and the unrelenting tears streaming down my cheeks conspired to blind me, but I managed to arrive at Jan's house safely. When she answered the door, I fell sobbing into her arms. Without a word of explanation from me, she knew what had happened.

About five years earlier, a mutual friend of ours had arrived at my door emotionally devastated because she had just learned her son was gay and that, as a young boy, he had been sexually molested by a trusted friend of the family and then drawn into homosexual activity with him. We had cried together, and then I just listened as she poured out her heartache over this revelation from her son. He was adamant that he would not testify against his abuser if the family tried to press charges, so legal action was not an option. At that time, I felt poorly equipped to give advice because I was so uninformed about the whole subject of "being gay." All I could do was empathize with her and promise to pray.

At the time my friend learned her son was gay, Dan was one of his friends. As the two grew into young adults, they stayed in contact and occasionally attended the same event. However, unbeknownst to me, my friend's son had said something to her in a recent conversation that led her to believe Dan was also gay. Uncertain as to whether she should tell me this troubling information, she decided as an alternative to share it with Jan. Not wanting to pass along what might only be secondhand speculation, Jan had instead prayed that if it were true, Dan himself would be the one to tell me.

Meanwhile, I had been troubled by a growing suspicion and concern that a close friend of our family had sexually molested Dan when he was a teenager. Wanting Jan's prayer support, I told her that I planned to question Dan that Easter Sunday about my concerns and asked her to be praying. What I didn't know was that she was already praying that if Dan was gay, he would tell me that afternoon. So when I appeared at Jan's door that Sunday night, she instinctively knew that God, in his sovereignty, had answered both of her prayers.

Between sobs, I haltingly shared with Jan my conversation with Dan from earlier that day. As I poured out my heart to her, I truly wanted to die. I could not see any hope in the future—only pain, loss, and unbearable loneliness. What I did not know and could not have even contemplated at that moment was that God did have a future for me, a future filled with his love and faithfulness. He was already working behind the scenes to provide encouragement and hope. This was especially evident that Sunday night when I arrived home.

On the previous Thursday, I discovered on the bookshelves in my guest room a book written by Elizabeth Elliott that I had not yet read. For years, I had regarded Mrs. Elliot as a spiritual mentor. God had used her books and other writings to minister to and encourage me at several crucial points in my life. I was surprised to find I had a book of hers I had not yet read since I usually read them as soon as I bought them. I placed the book on the nightstand by my bed, thinking, *I want to start reading this book.*

Returning home from Jan's that Sunday night, my mind was a jumble of thoughts and fears, and I doubted I would be able to go to sleep. As I prepared for bed, I saw the book by Mrs. Elliott on my nightstand, *A Path Through Suffering: Discovering the Relationship between God's Mercy and Our Pain.* I picked it up, and as I thumbed through it, glancing at the chapter titles, I knew God had saved that book for me to read at that particular time.

The theme of the book was how God allows dark, death-like situations into our lives so we can know through experience the life of Christ within us—the scriptural principle of life out of death. As I flipped through the book, a page where Mrs. Elliott emphasized the importance of learning to relinquish things to God caught my attention. The chapter was appropriately titled "Open Hands." I began reading:

> It is not the external circumstances themselves that enable us to reproduce the pattern of His death, but our willingness to accept the circumstances for His sake.

> Relinquishment is always a part of the process of maturing. When Christian parents have done all that can be done to shape their children for God, the time comes when the hands must let go.

The child, now a responsible adult, must be released. For any parent this is painful, even when the child is moving in the direction the parents prayed for.

When on the other hand, the child has obviously rejected what the parents have taught, the severing is painful in the extreme. All has been done that could be done and all has been done in vain. Nevertheless the time comes to let go, as it came for the father of the prodigal when he turned his wayward son over to God. He must have foreseen the direction he would take, but he prayed for him and waited every day for his return. God cared for that young man as the father could never have done, brought him to bankruptcy (another severe mercy), and returned him to his father, repentant and willing even to be a mere servant . . . [1]

I felt Elizabeth Elliott was personally sitting there talking to me, and through her, God was gently saying, "You've got to turn loose of Dan and trust me to work in his life."

The fear of losing him and of what lay ahead was overwhelming. The future looked dark, empty, and fearful—and I felt so alone. But God had already foreseen my fears, and at the top of the next page in the book, I read, "Do not fear what you are about to suffer . . ." (Revelation 2:10 NASB). Those words were so appropriate and so personal.

By my bedside that night, my heavenly Father assured me that I was not alone; he had promised he would never leave me or forsake me (Hebrews 13:5b NIV). Just as he had done in past painful situations, he would use this to draw me closer to himself and teach me to know him in a deeper way. The Lord reminded me of how he, in a redemptive way, had used my other times of painful loss to equip me to minister to others who were hurting. In that same way, he would use this difficult time to prepare me to help others who would walk down this same dark road.

But that night, being able to help others felt very remote and even impossible. I had to get myself together first; I had to find emotional healing, and I knew I had to learn everything I could about homosexuality. Until that day, homosexuality had been just a word, something I knew very little about—only that the Bible condemned it and it was something for which I felt a personal disgust. But now, homosexuality had a face—the face of my son.

Chapter 2

Reality Keeps Knocking at My Door

Reality greeted me when I awoke the next morning. The events of Sunday hung over me like a heavy, dark cloud that I had to grope through to start the day. God's faithful reassurances the night before had given me a small amount of peace, and surprisingly, I had fallen asleep without difficulty and slept soundly until the alarm woke me. But now, the day lay ahead like an uncharted course through dark waters, and I found myself wishing I could pull the covers over my head and stay in bed all day rather than face the waiting world.

I had to go to work. I could not in good conscience call in sick. After all, I was the business administrator at a large church, so pretending to be sick was a little unethical and inconsistent with my position. But, I reasoned, it would not be completely untrue; I did feel sick. My stomach was in knots, my head was pounding, and my emotions were in my mouth, threatening to spill out if I opened it to interact with people.

Actually, the greater pretense would have been to act as if everything was fine, including me. I certainly didn't intend to tell anyone what I had learned about my son. Most of the executive and office staff of the church had met him. He occasionally came to church with me, usually for one of the special events, and stopped by the office periodically. I wasn't sure how they would react toward him, or me for that matter, if they knew he was gay. It was increasingly clear. I could not tell anyone about Dan. Then the realization hit me:

Dan and I had changed places. He had come "out of the closet," but I was going in. By revealing his secret life to me, he had found some relief from his burden, but now it was my dark secret to carry. I had picked up the millstone, and it was one I could not ask others to help me carry.

In many ways, discovering your child is gay is initially a lot like a death in the family: the sense of unreality and numbness, the relentless pain, the shattered dreams, the loss of extended family through that child—all of which I experienced when my older son Nat was killed. But there is a major difference. This is a pain and loss often suffered in isolation, as there is no obituary notice, no friends gathering around to give comfort, no cards and notes of condolences, no flowers, no casseroles brought to your home because this is a loss that is difficult to share with others. You can hardly articulate the loss to yourself; how can you bear to put it into words to others?

I decided I would go to work, I would try to act normal, and I would say nothing. A fleeting thought passed through my mind. Maybe I would be killed in an accident on the way to work and whisked away to heaven where all tears would be wiped away and the future would be bright and beautiful! Although that picture was momentarily appealing, realistically I knew it was selfish, not thinking about the pain that would bring to Dan, and merely represented my grasping for a way of escape from my dilemma.

I stayed in my office that day as much as possible to avoid having to talk to people. I kept in place my "everything's fine" mask, but it was a fragile facade that I feared would slip at any moment. About mid-morning, Jan called to check on me, and her familiar and caring voice made the mask crumble.

"Get your things together. I'm coming to get you," Jan instructed. "You're in no condition to be at work today. I'll tell everyone you have to leave because you're sick."

Within a very short time, Jan arrived at my office. She helped me gather up my few things, put her arm around my shoulders, and walked me out of the church office. As we passed several people, she called over her shoulder, "Ann's not well. I'm taking her home," and out the door we went.

So there I was again, back at Jan's house, my safe haven. Jan was a long-time, close friend. Actually, we were more than friends; we were like sisters. We had been through a lot together over the years, and she was a strong Christian whom I could count on for encouragement and godly counsel. She was someone I could trust because I knew she loved and cared not only for me, but also for Dan. At that point, she was the only person I felt I could trust with all my fears, concerns, and questions.

Since my emotions were somewhat more under control than the night before, we were able to talk more extensively about the situation. What was I to do? As we talked, Jan remembered hearing a woman named Barbara Johnson on the radio the previous week sharing her story on *Focus on the Family* with Dr. James Dobson. Barbara Johnson's husband had been severely injured in a near-fatal car accident, the oldest of her four sons had been killed in Vietnam, a second son had been killed in a car accident in Alaska, and a third son had disappeared for a number of years into the gay culture. She had written a book telling of these losses and struggles and how especially devastating it had been for her when she discovered her son was gay. Her book was aptly titled *Where Does a Mother Go to Resign?* Mrs. Johnson's story and the title of her book struck a chord with me. Here was a mother who had walked this road ahead of me. I needed to find that book. Jan assured me she would try to find a copy.

I returned to work the next day, feeling better, and tried to concentrate on my responsibilities. The executive staff of the church had made plans to take the secretaries out to a local restaurant for lunch that day in observance of National Secretaries' Day. Since I supervised all the ladies in that position, I didn't see any way I could gracefully get out of going.

At the restaurant, nothing on the menu looked appealing. The thought of trying to swallow food almost nauseated me. I figured I needed to order something for the sake of appearance, so I ordered a small, light sandwich and managed to get a couple bites down before

I concluded I would gag if I took another bite. One of the ministers noticed I wasn't eating and politely inquired, "What's the matter, Ann? Something wrong with your sandwich?"

With a weak smile, I replied, "No, I'm just not hungry." Thankfully, he accepted that answer and said no more. Back at the office, the day dragged on endlessly. I just wanted to get out of there, away from people, and hide out in the seclusion of my home.

When the phone rang later that evening, I hesitated, not wanting to talk to anyone. I waited until it had rung a few times and then reluctantly picked it up. I was relieved to hear Dan's voice.

"Hi, Mom. I was just calling to see if you had slit your wrists yet." I realized Dan's morbid question was a joking way of showing his genuine concern about how his revelation had affected me. "I hadn't heard from you since Sunday. You hadn't called, and I was getting worried about you. Are you all right?"

"I'm okay," I responded quietly. "But, son, that was quite a bombshell you laid on me Sunday, and I have to be honest—this is really hard for me. It's going to take me awhile to absorb this and know how to respond. I do love you, Dan. I love you very much. But all my love can't call wrong right, and what you are doing is wrong. The way you are living is wrong."

Sadly, at that point in time, I was so immersed in my own pain and despair that I didn't have the appropriate understanding or concern about my son's longstanding painful struggle. The extent of how difficult it was for him to tell me he was gay and his agony over the possibility that his revelation might cause a wall of separation between us had not yet penetrated my own self-absorbed reaction. Nor had I considered what message my lack of contact with him since Sunday afternoon was communicating to him. My own pain was all-consuming. It was only later, when I began to learn more about my son's personal struggle and years of hurting, that my concern for him came into more proper perspective.

Later that evening, I was sitting at the kitchen table, reading my Bible, and trying to pray for Dan, but I was struggling. Whenever I started to pray, thoughts of his sexual behavior would spring up in my mind. Finally, I lowered my head into my hands, weeping, and cried out to the Lord, "Oh, God, I love my son so much, and the knowledge of his sinful lifestyle is ripping me apart. The pain is so deep I can hardly bear it."

Then, very gently, God impressed these piercing words upon my heart: "That's how *your* sin hurts me. I love you very much, and when you sin, it hurts me deeply, just the way your son's sin hurts you."

That sobering and humbling truth had never occurred to me, and it cut to the quick of my heart. I began to realize I had a lot to learn about God's love—for Dan and for me.

My immediate concern, however, was the quickly approaching weekend, which promised to bring further complications and more apprehension. I was scheduled to fly to Missouri for my annual April visit with my elderly mother, my siblings, and their families who lived in the area. The timing of my trip had been planned to coincide with the annual family reunion, where I would see lots of relatives. How could I function normally around them when my life felt so abnormal?

I would be staying with my mother in her small apartment. How could I hide from her my lack of appetite and my unpredictable emotional state? I could not tell her what I now knew about Dan, her grandson. Mother loved Dan very much, and it wasn't that I feared she would stop loving him. I knew she wouldn't, but I also knew that learning he was gay would be very traumatic for her, and at her age, I didn't want to inflict that struggle and pain on her life. I was blessed with a wonderful, godly mother who was an inspiration and strong influence on my life. She was a woman of prayer, and she prayed regularly for Dan. I knew this was too heavy a burden to lay on her, yet I wondered how I was going to be with her for ten days and hide from her what I was going through. And what would I say to family members when they asked about Dan and how he was doing?

Instead of looking forward to the trip home as I usually did, I was dreading it and fervently wished I wasn't going. But that was not an option. My only way to survive would be to depend on the Lord for strength each day, emotionally and physically, for wisdom about how to respond to people, and for his grace to sustain me.

Meanwhile, my faithful heavenly Father was already at work making provision for my trip. On Thursday, Jan called to tell me she had found a copy of Barbara Johnson's book *Where Does a Mother Go to Resign?* She had prayed the Lord would help her find the book in time for me to take it with me and, after phone calls to several Christian book stores, had located a copy. Ever the faithful friend, Jan immediately drove to the church to deliver the prized book so I would have it to read during my trip.

Waiting at the airport the next day, I began reading Barbara Johnson's book and continued reading it—or more accurately, devouring it—at every opportunity. Her book was my lifeline. Here was another mother who had experienced the same shock, pain, questions, and search for answers when she learned of her young son's homosexuality. Her book was a timely provision from my heavenly Father, bringing the counsel and encouragement I so desperately needed. I would later learn that this was not the only time he would use this special lady to minister to me.

Later, when I looked back over that week, I thought I should have won an academy award for my great acting. But I knew I could not take any credit for how well the week had gone; it was obviously God's wonderful grace and mercy that carried me through and enabled me to function normally. I talked and interacted with family members without arousing any suspicions; my emotions stayed under control, and I was able to eat enough that no one noticed my puny appetite. When anyone asked about Dan, I smiled and replied, "Oh, he's doing fine, thank you." But to myself, I would finish the sentence, *if you can call being gay "doing fine."*

There were times I almost said something about Dan to some of my family, but I kept questioning myself, "How will they respond if they know? Will they treat Dan differently?" I remembered Dan's tearful words to me that Sunday afternoon, "I was afraid you wouldn't love me anymore," and I could not risk the possibility that someone in my family might reject him if they learned he was gay.

In spite of all the Lord's faithful reassurances and demonstrations that he was with me and would continue to be there in the days to come, I kept slipping back into fearfulness and dread of the future. During those times, I even struggled with my attitude toward God. One night, within days of my return home, I found myself again in a black hole of despondency. I didn't know where to turn for answers; the future looked like a long, lonely, black road with no end in sight. Emotionally and mentally, I was in total despair and cried to the Lord, "Lord, I can't do this. I can't walk down this black road. Dan's all the family I've got left. You're asking too much of me; you've gone too far this time, God."

This was not the first time an unexpected heartache and crushing loss came crashing into my family. On another Easter Sunday, thirteen years earlier, my husband, who was the leader of a thriving Christian ministry at the time, unexpectedly died after a very brief illness. He was only forty-three. A number of years before that, between the birth of Dan and his older brother Nathan, we had lost a baby daughter through a pre-term delivery. Then, to compound those losses, just three-and-a-half years after my husband's death, Nat had been killed in a motorcycle accident the day after Christmas. He was only twenty-three. And now this—my one remaining child was identifying himself as gay and living in a homosexual relationship. How could I deal with one more family loss stacked on top of the previous losses? Couldn't God see that I had already suffered enough?

For a few brief moments, I just wanted to run away—run away from life and even run away from God. But in the midst of those dark thoughts, I knew God was saying to me, "And where will you go? Who will you turn to?"

I knew there was no place else to go, no one else to turn to. If I turned my back on God, I was turning away from my only source of hope and healing—for me and for my son. I knew that once again I needed to bow before the Lord in surrender to his sovereignty and love and accept what he was allowing to come into my life.

Our heavenly Father is so patient and long-suffering with us, his near-sighted children. In those previous times of great pain and loss, he taught me so much and in so many ways powerfully demonstrated his faithfulness and sufficiency. But now my eyes were focused only on this new pain of the moment, and I was not remembering the "treasures of darkness" he had given me in other dark times. "I will give you the treasures of darkness, riches stored in secret places, so that you may know that I am the LORD, the God of Israel, who summons you by name" (Isaiah 45:3).

Chapter 3

Learning to Love God's Way

Recorded in the Old Testament is the account of how God made a way for his people to cross the Jordan River when it was at flood stage. He miraculously caused the water to stop flowing upstream and to "pile up in a heap" a long distance from where the people needed to cross so that, under Joshua's leadership, they were able to walk across the riverbed on dry ground.

God commanded Joshua to instruct the priests to gather up twelve stones from the middle of the riverbed and carry them to the other side. Joshua then set up the stones as a lasting monument to the place where God had demonstrated his awesome power and might on behalf of his people. The "standing stones" were to be an ongoing memorial of God's faithfulness to make a way for his people when they were facing seemingly impossible situations. Repeatedly, God reminded his people to remember what great things he had done for them in the past.

But now I was failing to remember the "standing stones" in my own personal history. During the dark and painful days following the loss of my beloved husband and then the fatal accident of my firstborn son, God had never forsaken me. His Word was an instrument of encouragement, healing, and guidance. In many ways, he faithfully reassured me of his unfailing love and care and dramatically displayed his sovereignty in the circumstances of my life. In amazing ways, he wonderfully provided for me and at times demonstrated his ability to do what seemed impossible. He comforted me when I was grieving and lonely, made a way for me when the future was uncertain, and gave me the "treasures of darkness"—the joy of a growing intimacy with Jesus Christ. These were my "standing stones," memorials of God's faithfulness to me. Like Joshua's altar, my memorials were meant to be remembered and to build my faith for future trials. They were meant to prepare me for this moment.

My final response to this crisis of faith became the defining moment of my journey. So much of what God would do in the future went back to that moment, to my decision not to draw away from God in rebellion but to bow in submission.

Now, more than ever, it was essential for me to have a strong relationship with Jesus Christ and a confident, daily trust in him, not only for my own survival and spiritual growth but also for Dan's well-being. My own strength had already proven to be wavering, puny, and inadequate. I needed to live in the reality of Philippians 4:13: "I can do everything through him who gives me strength."

I had so much to learn and God was eager to teach me. He was impressing upon me the importance of continuing to demonstrate my love to Dan, and that it would be necessary for me to understand God's love in a deeper way. I opened my Bible to John 3:16, a very familiar verse I had memorized in childhood but needed to view with fresh eyes. "For God *so loved the world*, that he gave his one and only Son . . ." (emphasis added). God loved a very sinful world, and it was for sinful people that his Son Jesus came to die. Since childhood, I knew that included me, but now God wanted me to see the broader scope of his love and that Dan and all other homosexuals were a part of that world God loved and Jesus died for.

He also reminded me that his love was unconditional. He guided me to another familiar verse, Romans 5:8: "But God demonstrates his own love for us in this: While we were *still* sinners, Christ died for us" (emphasis added).

The sinful state of a person does not stop God from loving him or cause him to love the person any less. That was the kind of love I needed to have for Dan. But in spite of my good intentions and noble desires, the knowledge of my son's homosexuality threatened to put a wall between us—a wall built by me. When I thought about my son or tried to pray for him, a big wall appeared in my mind with the word HOMOSEXUAL written on it. I couldn't seem to get around it, so I prayed, "Lord, help me see Dan the way you see him." The Bible states that Jesus is the exact representation of God's being (Hebrews 1:3), so it seemed logical that the best place for me to see how God loved people was to look in the Gospels to see how Jesus treated people while he was on this earth.

First, I saw the attitude of Jesus toward "tax collectors and sinners" who were rejected and despised by both the religious leaders and common people alike. Luke 15:1 records, "Now all the tax collectors and the sinners were coming near him to listen to him" (NASB).

They not only came near Jesus to listen to him, but Mark 2 records that Jesus had dinner at a tax collector's house, and *many* tax collectors and "sinners" ate with him and his disciples. The result: Many of those tax collectors and sinners followed Jesus! I had read the Gospels many times, but now these verses jumped out at me. Contrary to how some in the Christian community were responding to those identifying themselves as "gay," and contrary to my own reservations, Jesus mingled with the sinners of his day, and *they* wanted to be with him and to listen to him. What if Jesus had not reached out to them and eaten with them? Would they have ever followed him?

Then there was the meeting between Jesus and the woman at Jacob's well, recorded in John 4. Jesus was sitting at the well, resting from a long, walking journey, when a Samaritan woman approached to draw water. Jews did not normally associate with Samaritans, but much to her surprise, Jesus immediately began a conversation. He amazed her even further by revealing his knowledge of her multiple marriages and that she was presently living with a man who was not her husband. Knowing this about her, he did not condemn her, but continued talking with her, offering her living water that could satisfy the inner spiritual thirsting of her soul. She came to believe that Jesus was the Christ, the promised Messiah, and many other Samaritans believed in Jesus because of her testimony. What if Jesus had shown the same attitude toward the Samaritan woman that other Jews normally exhibited? What if he had been disgusted by her lifestyle and avoided contact with her? She and many other Samaritans would never have followed Jesus.

But the most revealing portrayal of Jesus' heart was his encounter with the woman taken in adultery in John 8. The record is clear; there was no doubt of her guilt. The woman had been caught in the very act of adultery, a crime punishable under Jewish law by stoning. The motives of the Pharisees who brought her to stand before Jesus were obviously self-serving and left no room for compassion for the woman or concern about the guilt of the other party caught in the adulterous activity. The Pharisees thrust the woman before Jesus in front of all the people gathered to listen to him. They proclaimed their charges against her and demanded of Jesus, "Now what do you say?"

Jesus made no audible response to their question, but bending down, he began to write on the ground with his finger. In answer to their continuing questions, he straightened up and blindsided them with his penetrating statement: "If any one of you is without sin, let him be the first to throw a stone at her" (John 8:7). And one by one, her accusers quietly faded from the scene until the only one left facing the woman was Jesus. When Jesus asked her who remained to condemn her, she replied, "No one." Jesus' merciful, forgiving response was, "Then neither do I condemn you." But his gracious words were followed by an undeniable admonition. "Go now, and leave your life of sin" (John 8:11).

God was giving me a deeper understanding of his unconditional love for all people. He loved them as they were and where they were, but because of his love, he could not leave them there. He called them to leave a life of sin and enter into a new and changed life that could be found in him. God's lessons were piercing my heart and showing me the way I was to love Dan.

To be honest, I feared that my mother-love, strong as it was, would be insufficient and never measure up to the high standards of God's love. I felt incapable of the kind of love Jesus consistently showed to people who were caught up in sinful behavior. So my next prayer became: "Lord, give me your love for Dan. Love him through me."

God answered that prayer by pointing me to Romans 5:5, showing me that God's love was already residing in my heart. "Because God has poured out his love into our hearts by the Holy Spirit, whom he has given us."

I began seeing that a wall built of my own pride, self-righteousness, and unloving spirit was keeping God's love from overflowing to others. With God's help, I had to tear down that wall so his compassion and love could flow to others. The "wall of homosexuality" in my mind started crumbling as God continued teaching me what it meant to love Dan with his unconditional love.

However, to my initial dismay, learning to love my son with God's love was only the first step in learning to love God's way. God next impressed upon me that he wanted me to accept and love Dan's partner, Matt. Now honestly, my old self wanted to rise up and say, "Wait a minute, God. It's one thing for me to love my son unconditionally, but expecting me to love his partner the same way is totally different and probably impossible!"

I think in the back of my mind I was blaming Matt for Dan being involved in homosexuality. This obviously had to be somebody's fault. I was already struggling with my own load of guilt and needed someone else to share the blame. I had met Matt when he helped Dan move into the apartment they would share and had seen him a few other times when he had stopped by the house with Dan, but I had never really talked with him or spent any time with him and wasn't sure I wanted to. But God was on a mission to change my heart, and he presented a line of reasoning I could not refute. Simply put, he told me I had to be a tangible demonstration of God's love for Matt. How could Matt believe that God loved him if I, who claimed to know and walk with God, couldn't?

Before long, the perfect occasion presented itself. One day when Dan and I were talking on the phone, he mentioned that Matt's birthday was the following Saturday. So, with some trepidation, I invited Dan to bring Matt over for dinner Saturday night and offered to fix Matt's favorite meal for a birthday dinner. Dan, surprised by my invitation, said he would check with Matt and let me know.

Once I knew for sure they were coming, my nervousness increased. Seeing Matt as anyone but Dan's gay lover was hard for me, and the images that came to my mind were disturbing. Sitting together at the dinner table would be so awkward. What would we talk about?

By Saturday afternoon, I was an emotional wreck. My stomach was churning, my thoughts were all jumbled, and I lamented, "Father, if you don't come to my rescue, I'll never make it through this night."

In the midst of all this nervous angst, the phone rang. To my total shock, it was Barbara Johnson—*the* Barbara Johnson!—author of *Where Does a Mother Go to Resign?*, the first book I had read after Dan's shocking disclosure to me that he was gay, which turned out to be the first of several encounters with her, as God kept bringing her to my attention. The month following Dan's confession, I took a previously planned driving trip to visit a number of friends. I did not plan to share with any of them about Dan, but while talking with a close friend in Atlanta, I broke down and told her. And what should she give me but copies of two tapes by Barbara Johnson! My friend had picked them up at her church recently when a special guest spoke about a ministry to ex-gays. Then, while in Virginia, I was in the home of other long-time friends and decided to share with them my concerns about Dan. They immediately told me about Barbara Johnson, who had spoken at a special ladies' conference at their church, and gave me another one of her books, *Stick a Geranium in Your Hat and Be Happy*.

From the book and tapes, I learned that Barbara Johnson had established a ministry for Christian parents of gay children. She had named it "Spatula Ministries" because she had found that when Christian parents discovered their child was gay, you had to scrape them off the ceiling with a spatula. I could identify with that! Since she encouraged parents to write to her, I wrote her a long letter, pouring out my heart and sharing that I had invited Dan's partner Matt over for dinner. Not really thinking that she might actually call me, I had included my phone number at the end of the letter. But God's timing is incredible! Mrs. Johnson received my letter the *same* Saturday Matt was coming for dinner and decided to call me.

Once I recovered from the shock that an accomplished Christian author and speaker was actually on the phone, I shared with her my nervousness and agitated stomach. She encouraged me to not think of Matt only as my son's sexual partner but to see him as a young man my son cared about. He must have some qualities that had attracted my son to him; she encouraged me to try to focus on those things and extend gracious Christian hospitality to him.

The phone call was very helpful in settling my nerves. I committed the evening to the Lord and prayed that he would empower me to reach out in love to Matt.

Imagine my surprise when Matt walked in that night and handed me a CD by Sandi Patti, a very well-known Christian vocalist. He told me she was one of his favorite Christian artists. (I didn't know until later that Matt grew up in a Christian, churchgoing family, but when he told them he was gay, they had kicked him out of the home and wouldn't have anything more to do with him.) The CD played softly in the background as we ate dinner, providing an appropriate icebreaker and setting the tone for the evening.

Wanting Matt to feel welcome and at ease as much as possible under the circumstances, I tried to keep the dinner conversation relaxed and neutral, purposely avoiding the subject of homosexuality or Dan and Matt's relationship. I think Matt may have been as nervous about the evening as I was, but he did look more comfortable as the evening progressed. Overall, our time together went well, but since Matt and Dan left shortly after dinner, I wasn't sure what their perception was. I was relieved when Dan called me the next day and told me Matt enjoyed the dinner and was very appreciative that I prepared his favorite foods. Dan also wanted me to know how much it meant to him that I did this for Matt. As for me, the evening was a breakthrough in my attitude toward Matt. I could tell that God was helping me tear down the restraining wall in my heart piece by piece.

However, my desire to show unconditional love toward Dan raised a very important and troubling question that I struggled to answer. Regardless of what the culture might be saying about homosexuality, I knew the Bible condemned homosexual behavior as a sin. God had created the sexual union to be exclusively between a man and woman and then only within the confines of the marriage relationship. As a believer and follower of Jesus Christ, I was committed to the Bible as the authoritative standard of what was right and wrong, what was acceptable in God's sight, and what was sinful. Just because Dan was my son didn't make his homosexual behavior less wrong. I had assured Dan within days of his confession to me that I still loved him very much, but I had also stated quite clearly that all my love couldn't call wrong right and pointedly told him the way he was living was wrong. God had made it clear to me I was to show his unconditional love to Dan, but how could I do that without it communicating to him that his homosexual behavior was acceptable? By demonstrating love and acceptance of him as my son, would he interpret that as my acceptance of his homosexuality? Would he interpret my disapproval and rejection of his homosexual behavior as a rejection of him?

I feared that if I stood true to God's Word on this issue, it would drive a wedge between Dan and me, and the possibility of losing him or destroying the close relationship we had was tearing me apart. That was part of the blackness I feared, yet I knew in my heart my allegiance to God had to come first. I felt like I was walking a tightrope, trying to balance showing God's love to Dan without compromising the standard and authority of God's Word.

I saw in the Gospels that Jesus was somehow able to accomplish this. He had reached out in unconditional love to sinners, including dishonest tax collectors, the woman at the well with her multiple marriages and who was currently living with someone who was not her husband, and the woman taken in adultery, clearly communicating his acceptance of *them*. But in doing so, he never lowered God's standard of righteousness. That was a lesson I needed to learn from him. I needed his wisdom and direction on how to do this, and in the process, I had to trust him to protect my relationship with my son.

Though the Lord was opening my eyes to this truth, there was so much he still needed to teach me. There were questions yet unanswered in my mind. Didn't the Bible strongly condemn homosexuality and call it an abomination? Wasn't the city of Sodom in the Old Testament destroyed because of its rampant homosexual activity? Didn't the first chapter of Romans teach that sexual relations with the same sex were unnatural and condemned by God? Didn't the apostle Paul write to the church at Corinth that "homosexual offenders" would not inherit the kingdom of God? How could I reconcile those very strong biblical positions against homosexuality and the equally strong teaching of God's incomprehensible love for sinners? And how did both streams of truth fit into what I believed God was showing me was to be my attitude toward Dan and his partner? A deeper look into God's Word was needed to give me the answers to these questions.

Chapter 4

Letting the Bible Clarify Homosexual Issues

As a Christian, there was no question in my mind of the authority of God's Word in all areas and issues of life. That was already a settled matter in my own mind and heart. Christians are to be guided by the truths and standards set forth in the Bible and must seek to live a life worthy of the Lord and please Him in every way (Colossians 1:10). This means agreeing with God on what he says is wrong and intentionally choosing to do what he says is right. It was also my growing conviction that it was important for all Christian parents to have this same fundamental and crucial attitude toward God's Word if they were going to successfully navigate the uncharted waters of their child's announced gay identity and all the accompanying issues that arise from that situation.

But what I personally needed at this point was a deeper and clearer understanding of *all* the Bible had to say on the subject of homosexuality. I needed to know more than just the clear statements that the behavior was immoral and sinful. I also needed to understand their context and how I could defend with confidence their ongoing validity and truth against those who would discard them or minimize their relevance for our day. It was important for me to not compromise the Bible's unambiguous characterizations of same-sex behavior as sinful, yet at the same time unmistakably show the love of God toward people engaged in homosexual practices.

I was confident that expanded knowledge and a deeper understanding of God's Word would better equip me as a Christian parent to know how to love and interact with my son. In a broader sense, it would also give me the resources to take a strong but loving stand against the growing tide of cultural interpretations of homosexuality that is sweeping our country and even our churches.

We cannot blindly accept our culture's definition of right or wrong behavior because the Bible warns us that our culture can be upside down in its humanistic views. The prophet Isaiah warned against those who call "evil good and good evil" (Isaiah 5:20). As Christian parents, we can't bend the rules or change the definition of sin just because our son or daughter is involved in a particular sin.

Very likely we may have our own preconceived ideas and interpretations on the subject but have not examined whether they line up with the full teaching of God's Word. We may know or have heard a few Bible verses on homosexuality (primarily, that it is an "abomination") that have formed our opinion on what the Bible says on the issue. The problem is that one or two verses may not give us a complete understanding of what the Bible teaches about homosexuality or what the Christian's response should be to those with same-sex attractions or engaged in homosexual practices.

In addition, we are faced with others' strongly held but conflicting views about the morality of homosexuality. On the one hand, there is the small but very vocal group who, while asserting their church affiliation, strongly advocate misguided ideas and erroneous doctrine. They travel around the country, appearing at various events, and spewing a message of hate for homosexuals. They claim to speak for God as they hold up signs boldly declaring, "God hates fags!" and "Turn or burn!"

On the other hand, there are churches that strongly emphasize the love of God and believe it should be expressed by tolerance and inclusiveness toward those involved in homosexuality. They insist that Christians have no right to judge the behavior or lifestyles of others. They welcome not only to their membership but also to their pulpits and denominational leadership persons who are active in homosexual relationships, all in the name of inclusiveness and tolerance. Sadly, an increasing number of major denominations are changing their traditional positions on the immorality of homosexual behavior and are embracing a stance of love, inclusiveness, and tolerance that ignores biblical statements concerning right and wrong behavior.

The Metropolitan Community Church located in many of our larger cities proclaims itself as an inclusive church for gays and lesbians and has its own interpretation of the Scriptures dealing with homosexuality—or "gay theology" as it is sometimes called—to justify homosexual behavior as natural and acceptable to God. Its mantra is "God made me gay, it is a gift from him, and I am to celebrate who I am."

Faced with these conflicting views on the morality of homosexuality, if we want to know what God *really* has to say about the issue, we must come to His Word, laying aside our preconceived ideas and what those around us are saying, and honestly ask, "God, what does your Word teach about this issue?" We need to know truth or, as Christian apologist Francis Schaeffer put it, "true truth." A solid biblical understanding can then give us a secure foundation on which to make the many decisions we will face in our relationship not only with our son or daughter but with their partners and will provide guidance on how we should respond to the whole homosexual issue and those who identify themselves as gay. Because of the importance of a biblical perspective for this journey, I want to share at this point some of the information and biblical truths God showed me in my own search for understanding and "true truth."

It needs to be acknowledged upfront that there are only a few biblical texts that speak directly to homosexuality. However, it cannot be concluded that the limited number of specific biblical references to homosexual practices is an indication of their insignificance in God's view. The frequency of mention of a subject does not necessarily indicate its importance. There are other forms of sexual conduct that the Bible condemns (bestiality, prostitution, incest) and does not extensively or frequently reference, but we certainly would not conclude from their limited treatment that those forms of sexual conduct should be regarded as insignificant or acceptable. Both the Old and New Testaments, particularly the writings of the apostle Paul in the New Testament, clearly address homosexual behavior as sinful conduct, and Jesus—though not specifically speaking to homosexual practice by name—clearly describes God's design for sexual behavior, which excludes homosexual practices.

While there may be a limited number of Scriptures that specifically address homosexual practice, the Bible has much to say about sexual conduct in general, making unmistakably clear what is acceptable before God and what is not, both in examples of the conduct recorded of individuals and in the specific teaching of the Scriptures. If we are going to be honest in our search of the Scriptures, we have to acknowledge that the Bible has much more to say about equally sinful heterosexual behavior outside of marriage. Heterosexual sexual relationships outside of marriage are a much more *culturally* acceptable sin but are just as wrong from the biblical point of view. The Bible's teaching on homosexuality is part of its much broader teaching on God's original design for human sexuality and marriage as part of the creation covenant.

Before we proceed, it is important to briefly address and clarify a very important distinction between homosexual *behavior or practice* and homosexual *orientation* resulting in homosexual *desires or urges*. The Bible does not speak directly to homosexual orientation (motives or origins) but addresses the *behavior or practices* that may result from those same-sex attractions. Robert A. J. Gagnon, author of *The Bible and Homosexual Practice*, makes this important comment: "What matters is not what urges the individual feels, but what they do with the urges, both in their fantasy life, and in their concrete actions."[1]

This is not to ignore or minimize the reality of the complex, internal, and painful struggle of the person with homosexual attractions, and we will look at that more in depth in later chapters.

But it is important to keep in mind at this point that it is the behavior—*the practice of homosexuality*—that the Bible clearly addresses and condemns.

In seeking to know what the Bible teaches about homosexual practice, the first question we need to ask is, What was the original design and intent by God, the Creator, for mankind and for human sexuality? To answer that question, I want to reference Joe Dallas from one of his several books on homosexuality. A past president of Exodus International, Joe lectures extensively at churches and conferences, directs a biblical counseling practice in California, and has authored a number of books.

He addresses the issue of God's original design and intent in a clear and concise manner in his book *When Homosexuality Hits Home*. He lists several things we can know with certainty, based on the Bible's teachings:

We are *created beings*, created with a specific *intent* (see Genesis 1:26-2:23).

One of the basics of the Christian faith is the concept of created intent, which teaches that we are created by a Maker who had a specific *intention* for our life experiences in general and our sexual experiences in particular. This belief is a cornerstone for our position on homosexuality because it sets the standard by which we decide what is or is not moral. By this standard, questions of right versus wrong or normal versus abnormal are determined by whether or not a thing is in harmony with the intentions of the Maker. Our primary responsibility in life then is not to discover what feels natural to us or what seems right to us. That is secondary. What's primary is to discover and then comply with the intentions of our Creator.

The created intent for the expression of human sexuality is fulfilled within the covenant of a *monogamous* and *heterosexual* union (see Matthew 19:4-6).

When Jesus was questioned about the legitimacy of divorce, He answered plainly: God's original, created intention was that marriage be independent ("A man shall leave father and mother, and shall cleave to his wife"), monogamous ("What . . . God hath joined together, let not man put asunder"), and heterosexual ("[He] made them male and female"). We can conclude, then, that anything short of that or apart from this is outside the boundaries of God's intention.[2]

In this day of relativism and no moral absolutes, people often want to be their own plumb line for making moral decisions of right and wrong and do not acknowledge or accept the higher and absolute authority of God and his Word.

Shortly after my son revealed his new "identity" to me, he learned that Doug, a high school friend and former neighbor of ours, had also come out as being gay. When Dan broke up with Matt, he needed a roommate to share the rent, so he asked Doug to move in with him. They never became partners but had a somewhat shared compatibility because of their past friendship and present gay identities.

Since I knew Doug from our old neighborhood, I asked Dan to bring Doug with him to dinner one night. During our table conversation, I purposely avoided the subject of homosexuality, but Doug said something that brought up the subject. In responding to him, I unintentionally used the word *abnormal* to describe homosexual behavior. Doug immediately bristled and shot out the challenging question, "Who says it's not normal?"

My response came so quickly and naturally I had no time to think about it. I simply replied, "Well, since God created us, I think he has the right to say what's normal."

Interestingly, Doug made no comeback, and the conversation moved on. My response was a true statement, but what I did not understand at the time was that desires and attractions to the same sex may seem very normal to the person who has struggled with them as long as he or she can remember.

God's original design and intent for man, as portrayed by Adam and Eve, was that man and woman would live together and become "one flesh" in their relationship. God's instructions for them were to be fruitful and multiply—to bear children. God designed mankind's sexuality for procreation and for pleasure (Genesis 2:24; 1:28a; Proverbs 5:15-19), and his creative intent was clearly for sexual intimacy to be expressed between a man and a woman within the relationship of marriage. God's intent has not changed since creation.

A book referenced earlier, *The Bible and Homosexual Practice*, authored by Robert Gagnon, assistant professor of New Testament at Pittsburg Theological Seminary, is a very scholarly, extensive, and in-depth study of the texts and hermeneutics of the Scriptures referencing homosexual practices in both the Old and New Testaments. Gagnon presents very strong arguments that show God's original intent for human sexual behavior and how homosexual practice violates that intent and therefore is sin:

> Scripture rejects homosexual behavior because it is a violation of the gendered existence of male and female ordained by God at Creation. Homosexual intercourse puts males in the category of females and females in the category of males, insofar as they relate to others as sexual beings. That distorts the sexuality intended by God for the health and vitality of the human race. God intended the very act of sexual intercourse to be an act of pluralism, embracing a sexual "other" rather than a sexual "same."[3]

Same-sex intercourse represents a suppression of the visible evidence in nature regarding male-female anatomical and procreative complementarity.[4]

The Bible presents the anatomical, sexual, and procreative complementarity of male and female as clear and convincing proof of God's will for sexual unions. Even those who do not accept the revelatory authority of Scripture should be able to perceive the divine will through the visible testimony of the structure of creation.[5]

Not only do we need to see from Scripture God's creative intent for mankind and human sexuality, but we also need to factor in the Fall of man and its tsunami impact on all mankind. When Adam and Eve disobeyed God's command in the garden to not eat the fruit of the Tree of Knowledge of Good and Evil, they introduced sin and death into the world, plunging themselves and all mankind born after them into a sinful state with a sinful nature (Genesis 2:16-17; 3:6-7; Romans 5:12). Joe Dallas makes clear some of the ramifications of the Fall as it relates to mankind in his explanation of what we can know with certainty from the Scriptures:

> **We are a *fallen race*, and the Fall has marred every part of our experience, including our sexual experience (see Psalm 51:5; Romans 5:12-19).**
>
> Paul's teaching in Romans 5, combined with David's remarks about his inherited sinfulness, is crucial to our understanding of homosexuality, even though the subject isn't mentioned in these Scriptures. They explain why some things that are sinful may feel perfectly natural and good to us, while things that are right in God's sight may feel, to us, unnatural and difficult. We are a fallen race, beset with any number of sinful tendencies. Further, the

Fall expresses itself differently through different people. We share a common curse in that each of us is born with a sin nature. But how that nature expresses itself is unique to the individual, leaving some people with a strong tendency toward violence, some with a weakness for lying and still others with unnatural sexual tendencies.

Homosexual behavior is both a *manifestation* of fallen nature and a *violation* of created intent (see Leviticus 18:22; 20:13; Romans 1:26-27; 1 Corinthians 6:9-10; 1 Timothy 1:9-10).

Many sexual behaviors are mentioned and condemned in both Testaments: adultery, incest, fornication, prostitution, and homosexuality are the most prominent. In light of the clear standard Christ set for human sexuality, these behaviors logically fall short of created design and are listed as moral violations in the Levitical law and in Paul's writings to the Corinthians and Timothy. Likewise, homosexuality is described in Paul's letter to the Romans as being unnatural and symptomatic of the larger problem of man's rebellion.[6]

As Dallas points out, homosexuality is one of many sexual behaviors that are identified and condemned as sinful by God in *both* the Old and New Testaments. Why, then, does homosexual behavior seem more sinful or abhorrent to us, especially to parents, than the sexual sins of adultery or fornication (sex outside of marriage)? Why is it that a son sleeping or living with his girlfriend or a daughter engaging in sexual activity with her boyfriend does not seem equally as sinful to us as a son or daughter involved in a homosexual relationship when God calls them all sinful?

When it comes to sexual sins, same-sex intercourse is often viewed as more offensive to Christians and even many non-Christians because it is seen as an *unnatural* sexual relationship, an obvious ignoring and rejection of the God-created and God-ordained roles of males and females in sexual relationships. It is a violation of his established order for human sexuality. As Dallas states, it is "symptomatic of the larger problem of man's rebellion" against God and his design and intent for mankind.

So how should we view the sin of homosexuality in comparison to other sexual sins? First, we must recognize that all sexual behavior that God calls sinful we must also call sinful, whether it is sexual intimacy with the opposite sex outside of the marriage relationship or sexual intimacy with the same sex. What the Bible calls sin, we must call sin.

We must be careful not to view some sexual sins as *more acceptable* (sexual intimacy between those of opposite sex outside of marriage) because they are *less offensive* (than homosexual intimacy) to us and thus, in our view, less sinful. All sexual sins violate the boundaries God has established for the expression of human sexual activity and behavior. For the Christian, sexual sin has an added dimension. The apostle Paul points out that all other sins a person commits are *outside* his body, but "he who sins sexually sins against his own body" because the Christian's body is a temple of the Holy Spirit (1 Corinthians 6:18-19).

Let's examine more closely some previously mentioned Scripture passages that clearly address homosexual behavior. Romans 1:26-27 speaks most directly and clearly to the unnatural nature of homosexual acts for both male and female:

> Even their women exchanged natural relations for unnatural ones. In the same way the men also abandoned natural relations with women and were inflamed with lust for one another. Men committed indecent acts with other men, and received in themselves the due penalty for their perversion.

To the heterosexual, the physical attraction of males or females to their own sex is so completely foreign to their own sexual desires and understanding that it can easily magnify the sin of homosexuality in their eyes.

The use of the word *abomination* in some Old Testament Scripture verses when referring to sexual relations with the same sex may also influence our view of homosexual behavior as especially sinful. The two most-quoted Old Testament passages regarding homosexual behavior are from Leviticus: "You shall not lie with a male as one lies with a female; it is an abomination" (18:22 NASV) and "If a man lies with a male as he lies with a woman, both of them have committed an abomination (20:13 NKJV).

In these verses, some translations of Scripture use the word *detestable* instead of *abomination*, but the words are very similar in meaning. *Merriam-Webster's Collegiate® Dictionary* gives the following definitions: "Abomination: extreme disgust and hatred: loathing" and "Detestable: arousing or meriting intense dislike: abominable."[7]

Some people may read those definitions and think, *Yep, that describes exactly how I feel about homosexuals!* And, to be honest, it's easy to say that with an air of superiority and self-righteousness. We would certainly never be involved in a behavior that God describes in those strong words. I have to confess those were my exact thoughts when I first heard those shocking words from my son, "Mom, I'm gay."

But it is usually a surprise to people, and maybe even a shock to some, to learn that God uses the same words elsewhere in his Word to describe actions and attitudes that we may be guilty of but view as much less serious sins. Following are a few other biblical references where God describes more familiar actions or attitudes as "abominations" or "detestable":

- Proverbs 11:1; Deuteronomy 25:16: *Dishonest scales/balances—* Dishonesty in our dealings with others.
- Proverbs 12:22: *Lying lips—*Have we never told a lie, not even a little "white" lie?
- Proverbs 16:5: *The proud of heart—*Pride is one of the seven things that God "hates" and are "detestable" to him, as listed

in Proverbs 6:16-19. Can any of us say we never entertain proud, self-centered thoughts or think we are better than someone else?

Pride is one of those very subtle sins that we are not always quick to acknowledge in our own hearts, but even if we do, we tend to be even more reluctant to view our pride the same way God does—as an abomination, detestable in his sight, and something he hates.

In the New Testament, 1 Corinthians 6:9-10 is often pointed to as a "proof-text" of the greater sinfulness of homosexuality:

> Do you not know that the wicked will not inherit the kingdom of God? Do not be deceived: Neither the sexually immoral nor idolaters nor adulterers nor male prostitutes nor *homosexual offenders* nor thieves nor the greedy nor drunkards nor slanderers nor swindlers will inherit the kingdom of God (emphasis added).

Obviously, these verses clearly state that the "homosexual offender" will not "inherit the kingdom of God"; in other words, they won't go to heaven. Some interpret these verses to mean such persons are not even eligible for God's redemption. But if we interpret this passage that way, we must also exclude from eligibility for heaven or salvation all those who commit any of the other sins identified in that passage—other sexual sins, i.e., adultery and fornication, as well as thieves and those who are greedy, get drunk, slander others (gossip), swindle (take advantage of others), or have any kind of idol in their life that comes between them and God. All are listed right along with the "homosexual offenders."

Verse nine does state emphatically "the *wicked* will not inherit the kingdom of God" (emphasis added). Other versions of the Bible translate the word *wicked* as "unrighteous" or "wrongdoers." Actually, since all of us initially fall into this category and are sinners by God's definition (Romans 3:11-14, 23), none of us will "inherit the kingdom of God" unless we come as repentant sinners to the foot of the cross and trust the redemptive work of Christ on our behalf for forgiveness and acceptance into God's kingdom. Whoever does come on that basis to God will be welcomed into his kingdom (John 3:16), and "whoever" includes the homosexual offender.

Please don't misunderstand what I am saying in regard to the sinfulness of homosexual behavior. The Bible teaches plainly in both the Old and New Testaments that homosexual behavior is a serious sin, and my intent is not to minimize that sin. My clarification is not that we should lower our view of the sinfulness of homosexual behavior but rather that we should raise our view of the seriousness of all other sins. Sometimes we Christians tend to categorize sin from very minor sins—such as gossip, a spirit of superiority to others, self-centeredness, jealousy, half-truths, a proud spirit, stirring up dissension and division among believers, disobeying God's Word—to the really big sins—such as adultery, murder, pedophilia, and maybe homosexuality close to the top of the list. Initially, the sin of homosexuality certainly ranked high on my list of sins with my proud, self-righteous attitude at the bottom, if it made the list at all. Early in my journey, I discovered that God had a lot of work to do in my own heart. In reality, because God is a holy God, *all* sin is offensive to God. The sacrificial and excruciating death of Christ on the cross was required to provide atonement and secure forgiveness for even our "smallest" sins. All sin brings pain to the heart of God. As Genesis 6:6 says, "The LORD was grieved that he had made man on earth, and his heart was filled with pain."

Before we stand in judgment as to who is the worst sinner, we need to examine our own hearts in the light of God's holiness and the measuring rod of his Word. The strongest words of condemnation uttered by Jesus were to the self-righteous religious leaders of his day. Imagining the following harsh and stinging words of Matthew 23:27-28, directed to the Pharisees and teachers of the law, coming from the mouth of Jesus may be hard for us:

You hypocrites! You are like whitewashed tombs, which look beautiful on the outside but on the inside are full of dead men's bones and everything unclean. In the same way, on the outside you appear to people as righteous but on the inside you are full of hypocrisy and wickedness.

To emphasize the sin of self-righteousness before God, Jesus told the parable of the Pharisee and the tax collector. Noteworthy is the way the parable is introduced in Luke 18:9-11:

> *To some who were confident of their own righteousness and looked down on everyone else,* Jesus told this parable . . . "Two men went up to the temple to pray, one a Pharisee and the other a tax collector. The Pharisee stood up and prayed *about himself: 'God, I thank you that I am not like other men—robbers, evildoers, adulterers—or even this tax collector . . .'"* (Emphases added)

In contrast, the tax collector (viewed as a "sinner" by most Jews) prayed in this manner: *"But the tax collector stood at a distance. He would not even look up to heaven, but beat his breast and said, 'God, have mercy on me, a sinner'"* (Luke 18:13, emphasis added).

Jesus commented regarding the tax collector, "I tell you that this man, rather than the other, went home justified before God" (Luke 18:14). This parable speaks volumes about our need to examine the attitude of our own hearts before the Lord and our attitude toward others.

God reminds us in 1 Samuel 16:7 that he always looks at the contents of our hearts. "The LORD does not look at the things man looks at. Man looks at the outward appearance, but the LORD looks at the heart."

Wrong Responses and Attitudes from Christians

This may be a good place to briefly address the sad fact that some Christians and churches have communicated a message of condemnation without love to the homosexual community. (I am humbly remembering I was once in that group or at least standing on the periphery of it.) We have been rather lopsided in our adherence to the often glibly quoted cliché, "Love the sinner, but hate the sin." We are heavy on hating the sin, but much lighter, if at all, on loving the sinner.

In fact, those who seek to minister to the homosexual community have told me that it's best for Christians to throw out that old cliché when speaking to or about those identifying themselves as homosexuals. Randy Thomas, formerly a staff member with Exodus International and one of the authors of *God's Grace and the Homosexual Next Door,* points out:

> You are dealing with a subculture that identifies as "gay." *They are identifying themselves by homosexuality.* To say that you *hate* homosexuality but love homosexuals doesn't make sense to those whose primary identity lies with their sexuality . . . The underlying difference that "hate the sin, love the sinner" completely misses is that the Christian sees homosexuality as a condition to overcome whereas the gay-identified person sees homosexuality as an *innate identity* he or she has embraced.[8]

Sadly, many Bible-believing churches (and individual Christians) have exhibited only a condemning, judgmental attitude toward the homosexual. There has been no demonstration in their words or actions of the love of God for them. Some persons, formerly active in the homosexual community, have shared the following reaction when they saw the hate-filled signs or heard the unloving, condemning statements of professing Christians: "If people like you are going to be in heaven, I don't want to go there!"

Many otherwise theologically sound and conservative churches fall into the category described by Mona Riley and Brad Sargent as "judgmental churches."

> Though standing for truth, judgmental churches give the law so forcefully that their members forget to mix in Christ-like love that exhibits itself in compassion, patience and willingness to help personally those who deeply desire transformation in their sexuality... The judgmental church has... somehow forgotten that although people are hopelessly mired in sin and fail to keep God's law, God's ever-present love and compassion have made a path for forgiveness through the death of His Son, Jesus Christ. For this reason, people justifiably call the judgmental church hypocritical. Judgmental Christians only rescue the perishing if they can ensure their life preservers will come back clean and in good repair. It is not enough that this church knows God's truth if they do not also display God's compassion and mercy.[9]

Robert Gagnon, along with his convincing scriptural arguments for the sinfulness and unnaturalness of homosexual practice, gives a very compassionate word of instruction and caution to the Christian and the church:

> A rigorous critique of same-sex intercourse can have the unintended effect of bringing personal pain to homosexuals, some of whom are already prone to self-loathing. That is why it needs to be emphatically stated that to feel homosexual impulses does not make one a bad person. I deplore attempts to demean the humanity of homosexuals . . . The person beset with homosexual temptation should evoke our concern, sympathy, help, and understanding, not our scorn or enmity. Even more, such a person should kindle a feeling of solidarity in the hearts

of all Christians, since we all struggle to properly manage *our* erotic passions. A homosexual impulse, while sinful, cannot take shape as *accountable* sin in a person's life unless one acquiesces to it. Thus a reasoned denunciation of homosexual behavior and all other attempts at nurturing and justifying homosexual passions is *not,* and should not be construed as a denunciation of those victimized by homosexual urges, since the aim is to rescue the true self created in God's image for a full life. (Emphasis added)[10]

Often wrong attitudes on the part of the church or individual Christians toward the gay community stem from misinformation or a lack of information about homosexuality combined with a faulty attitude. The church or individual Christians need to acquire accurate information about homosexuality and allow God to change their hearts and attitudes as they see more clearly his deep love for all the "whosoevers" of the world.

We need to be a living demonstration of God's love to those around us, especially to those either struggling with homosexual attractions or those actively engaged in homosexual behavior. The Bible gives a very clear description of God's love:

This is how God showed His love among us: He sent His Son into the world that we might live through Him. This is love: not that we loved God, but that he loved us, and sent His Son as an atoning sacrifice for our sins. (1 John 4:9-20)

Romans 5:8 further emphasizes the depth of God's love. "While we were *still* sinners, Christ died for us" (emphasis added).

Often Christians make the mistake of trying to convince gays and lesbians that their homosexual behavior or lifestyle is wrong and sinful before God. The greatest need of the homosexual person is not to change their homosexual practices; their greatest need is for a Savior. Jesus Christ is the only one who can provide forgiveness for their sins; give them a new, clean heart; and empower them to live a changed, holy life and be all God created them to be.

Arguments from the Other Side

Some of the limited number of passages in the Bible that deal directly with homosexuality along with their interpretation have generated questions and debate as to their meaning or application to us today. The proponents of homosexuality argue that Scriptures condemning homosexuality are misunderstood, incorrectly translated, are no longer culturally relevant for our day, or do not apply to monogamous, loving relationships.

Some of the most frequently disputed Scriptures are the historical account of the story of Sodom and Gomorrah (Genesis 19), the Levitical moral law that prohibited homosexual acts (Leviticus 18:22), and the references in the New Testament directly addressing homosexual behavior from the apostle Paul's writings, primarily Romans 1:26-27. Today, advocates of homosexuality frequently use their interpretation of these passages to defend the acceptability of homosexual behavior while at the same time disparaging the authority of the Scriptures. It is important to note that their arguments against the traditional interpretation of these passages are not just a rejection of biblical revelation and authority over sexual morality but of all divine revelation recorded in the Bible and any authority that it has over our lives today.

Rather than attempting in this book to present an explanation or interpretation in defense of the authority and relevance of these Scriptures for our day, I want to defer to other Christian writers who are much more qualified to write in depth on these passages and to refute the arguments by those advocating the moral and cultural legitimacy of homosexual behavior.

- Joe Dallas: *The Gay Gospel? How Pro-Gay Advocates Misread the Bible*

- Michael R. Saia: *Counseling the Homosexual*, Chapter 5, "What Does the Bible Say?"
- Don Schmierer: *An Ounce of Prevention*, Chapter 4, "What Would Jesus Say?" pp. 79-82
- Robert A. J. Gagnon: *The Bible and Homosexual Practice* (Dr. Gagnon's 493-page book contains an in-depth treatment and exegesis of all the scriptural passages that in any way refer to same-sex practices and capably refutes the interpretations and arguments of the advocates of homosexual relationships and activity.)

A Search and a Choice

Bob Davies, a former president of Exodus International, who as a Christian young man had his own personal internal struggles with same-sex attractions, needed to know for himself what the Bible really said about homosexuality. Was all homosexual behavior forbidden? Or just gang rape and promiscuous relationships without love and commitment?

> As an eighteen-year-old college freshman, I discovered an impressive array of books on homosexuality at the university library. Some of these books presented the subject of homosexuality from a "religious" point of view, although all of them were favorable toward adopting homosexual practice as a normal lifestyle . . . One Saturday morning, I was lying in bed reading one of these theological treatises on homosexuality. As I read page after page of arguments justifying same-sex practices, my mind wanted so much to believe the words I was reading. *If only I could really embrace this viewpoint, I thought, all of the conflict I feel inside would be resolved* . . . But, as hard as I tried to block it out, a stronger conviction refused

to budge from my conscience: *This book is wrong. These arguments are wrong. Homosexuality is wrong!* . . . Tears of frustration came to my eyes as I realized that no matter how much time I spent reading why homosexuality was an acceptable option for the Christian, I would never be able to believe it. I knew too much about the biblical stand on sex outside of marriage. Whether sex occurred between an unmarried man and woman or between two same-sex partners, the activity would always be fornication or adultery. No amount of justification or argument would change God's standard . . . So I had a clear choice to make: Would I obey God's Word, or seek to reinterpret it in order to fulfill my sexual desires?[11]

Some Important Distinctions

In reviewing what the Bible has to say about the sinfulness of homosexuality, we must recognize a couple of very important distinctions that the Bible makes. Let's look again at the verses from Leviticus listed earlier in this chapter.

> You shall not lie with a male as one lies with a female; *it* is an abomination. (Leviticus 18:22 NASV, emphasis added)

> If a man lies with a male as he lies with a woman, both of them *have committed* an abomination. (Leviticus 20:13 NKJV, emphasis added)

Note in the first passage, the word *abomination* is used to describe the *act* of sexual activity between same sexes, not the *persons* committing the act. The sinful act itself God condemns as an abomination, and there were serious consequences for those committing it then just as there were serious consequences for committing certain other sins. That principle is still true in our society today. The penalty (consequence) of breaking some laws is greater than the penalty for breaking other laws. But we are lawbreakers if we break *any* law, regardless of the degree of the consequences (James 2:10).

As I stated earlier in this chapter, it is also important to remember that the Bible does not address the issue of same-sex orientation, attraction, or desire for the same sex. Nowhere does the Bible call same-sex attraction a sin. It is *acting* upon those attractions, making the choice out of those attractions to engage in *sexual behavior* with an individual of the same sex that is labeled sin and condemned by God. Compare this to a man being attracted to a woman or a woman being attracted to a man. The attraction itself is not wrong. But when the individual *chooses* to move past recognizing that the person is attractive and perhaps desired to beginning to *entertain* lustful or covetous thoughts about that person or pursue lustful fantasies, he or she has *chosen* to engage in thoughts that God labels sinful. This is true of either the homosexual or heterosexual person. The attraction to the same sex or opposite sex can progress to entertaining lustful thoughts and, if not checked, to sinful sexual behavior.

While it is difficult for the heterosexual person to understand how any person could be attracted to his own gender, the attraction is very real for persons with a same-sex orientation. We should not be too quick to condemn them for the attraction without understanding the psychology of homosexuality and how those attractions can develop.

The question that swirled in my mind and demanded an answer was, How in the world did my son develop same-sex attractions that eventually led to same-sex behavior?

Chapter 5

Searching for Answers

Troubling Questions

When Dan dropped the emotional bombshell on me that Sunday afternoon, disclosing his same-sex attractions and homosexual involvement, the impact shattered my familiar world and quickly revealed to me how ill-equipped I was as a Christian mother to cope with this foreign subject. Questions with no immediate answers swirled around in my head and with each lap felt like razor-sharp arrows piercing my heart.

What else did I not know about my son? Did homosexuals approach or "come on" to other young men? *All* other young men? (Later my son would tell me that gays have what they call "gay-dar." They can sense if another man has homosexual attractions. So much to learn!) When I saw two young men walking down the street together, the question would flash through my mind, "I wonder if they are gay?"

I would later learn that my questions and pain were not unique, and that most parents agonize over these same questions when they learn their child or other family member has identified him- or herself as gay and perhaps already involved with a same-sex partner. Individual circumstances may vary, but the haunting and troubling thoughts are much the same.

When parents first learn of their child's gay identity and same-sex behavior, the most immediate and disturbing question seems to be, "How could *my* child be gay?" That was certainly my foremost thought. Dan's father and I had publicly dedicated him to the Lord when he was a baby and committed ourselves to raise him in the "training and instruction of the Lord" (Ephesians 6:4b). Even the meaning of the name we gave him reflected our desires for him—Daniel, "friend of God." As a young child, Dan had made a profession of faith in Christ as his Savior. On many of his craft items, he had, with great care, intentionally placed the acronym PTL (Praise the Lord). He had sat in on group Bible studies taught by his father in our home, dutifully underlining passages of Scripture in his Bible. How could he now be gay? What had gone wrong?

Feelings of guilt and shame consumed me. Where had my husband and I failed as parents? Out of my sense of failure, I cried out to God, "One of the most important jobs you gave me was to raise a godly son, but somehow I botched that!" My feelings of failure as a Christian parent were like a heavy weight of condemnation on my back, for I concluded that if others knew about Dan, they, too, would view me as a very poor Christian parent.

Without any words from me, Dan must have sensed that I would struggle with this, because a few days after our initial conversation, he tried to assure me. "Mom, please don't blame yourself. It's not your fault for who and what I am."

But still I thought it must be. How did a seemingly normal little boy or teenager develop an abnormal attraction for his own sex? How could my handsome son, who had gone steady with a girl for three years during his late teens, now be physically and emotionally attracted to his own sex? Dan claimed he was born that way, but I couldn't accept that. Wasn't that just propaganda promoted by the gay community that he now accepted as true? I tried to remember all the supporting arguments Dan had presented that Sunday afternoon when he, out of his personal pain, revealed the sexual identity he had embraced and the secret life he was living. It was obvious he was sincere in what he believed about homosexuality, and I didn't have the understanding or accurate information I needed to refute his statements. I could only stand on what I did know with certainty—the clear position of Scripture that homosexual behavior was not God's divine plan for human sexuality and was condemned in the Scriptures as immoral and sinful behavior. I desperately needed to find answers to my troubling questions, and I knew the answers had to be based on true and accurate information about homosexuality from a Christian perspective.

An Important Foundation

In retrospect, I can see how the Lord faithfully laid down an important and necessary foundation on which to begin my search for information. He first began to deal with issues and sinful attitudes in my own heart. He lay bare my deep prejudices and pride. He showed me that I did not understand his heart in this issue, that I needed to know his love in a deeper, experiential way, and then learn how to walk in that love on this new journey.

Increasingly, I saw the Lord's wisdom in first strengthening the bond of love from me toward my son. Being able to show love and acceptance to my son instead of condemnation and rejection was keeping the door of communication open between us. This provided opportunity for conversations with Dan that otherwise would not have been possible, and our relationship grew more open and honest than it previously had been. As Dan became more certain of my now unconditional love, he felt more liberty to share his views, thoughts, and even his struggles with me. Though God was teaching me the importance of loving Dan with his unconditional love, I had never used those precise words—*unconditional love*—to Dan. One day he surprised me by saying, "Mom, I know you love me unconditionally, and I know that the way I am living is causing you pain, and I'm sorry about that. But I have to live my own life. I have to make my own choices."

I was able to answer him quietly and gently, "I know that, son, but you must also be prepared for the consequences of your choices because every choice has a consequence."

Dan and I were all that was left of our immediate family, and thankfully, he wanted to preserve our close relationship as much as I did. But now we both had to learn how to do that under these new circumstances. I had already seen in Matt's situation that when a son or daughter came out, not all parents and children reacted toward each other the way Dan and I were. Sometimes, out of shock, anger, and pain, hurtful words are spoken. Immediate reactions and quick decisions can badly damage relationships, which are not quickly or easily restored.

A New Relationship

If you are reading this book, it is probably because you, too, are looking for answers about what to do now that your child or perhaps another family member has labeled him- or herself as gay. Before I share the results of my search for information and answers, I want to summarize some important guidelines I discovered I needed to follow in this new relationship with my son.

- Make it your first priority to strengthen your own personal relationship with God through time in his Word and in prayer. You will need his guidance, wisdom, strength, direction, encouragement, perseverance, and hope for this journey. Let God reveal to you your own sins and faults, and honestly deal with them when he does.
- Love your child unconditionally. As I shared earlier, God can give you the ability to love your child with his love. Communicate that unconditional love regularly to your child in ways that he or she can understand. Assure him or her of your care. He or she is still your child; that has not changed. What has changed is what you now know about him or her. He or she needs to know that your love is not based on his or her acceptable or unacceptable behavior but on the fact that he or she is your child.

- Unconditional love does not mean condoning wrong and sinful behavior. You can accept your child without accepting his or her unacceptable behavior. The age and circumstances of your child will determine how you deal with his or her unacceptable behavior.
- Stand true to biblical truths regarding sin. But understand that homosexuality is not the greatest sin nor is it the only sin the Bible calls "an abomination." In the book of Proverbs, dishonesty, lying, and pride are all named as "abominations" to the Lord (KJV) and in 1 Corinthians 6:9, thieves, drunkards, greed, and gossip are all listed next to homosexual activity as sinful. Even *our* "smallest" sin required Jesus' death on the cross as payment for that sin. It is the *sin* that is an abomination to God, not the *person* committing the sin.
- Don't preach to your son/daughter about the wrongness of homosexual behavior every time they walk in the door. Barbara Johnson gave parents this very succinct advice: "Shove a sock in your mouth! They heard you the first time."[1]
- Ask God to help you also love your child's partner. His or her partner is someone he or she cares about and is significant to him or her. But more importantly, he or she is someone who needs to see Christ's love demonstrated through you. Initially, you may not want anything to do with the partner, let alone love him or her. But be open to what, in time, God might want you to do and therefore enable you to do.
- Be very intentional about ways to find resources that will help you on this journey. Learning all you can from a Christian perspective about the homosexual condition will help you know and understand the pain that is in your child's life. The more I learned about some of the factors that can contribute to the development of same-sex attractions and the pain that my son had experienced, the more my heart began to melt and my compassion grew for my son. Sy Rogers, an internationally known Christian communicator specializing

in sexual and relationship issues within the church, often makes this statement in his presentations: "Learning accurate information about homosexuality does not make homosexual behavior less wrong; but it does make it more understandable."

- Many parents feel the need for professional help to provide guidance and support, and I would certainly recommend and encourage this. Be very sure, however, that you seek out a Christian counselor who will provide counsel from a biblical, Christ-centered approach. Also, finding a counselor who has some knowledge of and counseling experience in same-sex orientation is very helpful. A word of caution: Please don't assume at this point that if you can just get your child to go to a Christian counselor, the counselor can "fix" him or her. If your loved one is open to seeing a Christian counselor, fine. But don't see this as a quick and permanent solution to "straightening out" your kid. Again, it is vitally important that the counselor be one who has knowledge and counseling experience in same-sex attractions. The wrong counselor can cause more harm than help.

- Find sources of support. Restored Hope Network *(www.restoredhopenetwork.com)* is a network of Christian ministries reaching out in grace and truth to those struggling with unwanted same-sex attractions or wanting to leave a homosexual lifestyle. They provide a biblical approach to homosexual issues and offer support groups for strugglers and families affected by homosexuality. Harvest USA *(www.harvestusa.org)* is a long-established ministry that ministers to those struggling with same-sex attractions. Another resource is Living Hope Ministries *(www.livinghope.org)*. Waiting Room Ministry *(www.WaitingRoomMinistry.org)* offers onsite parent support groups in some locations and online resources for parents in underserved areas. An additional ministry I would recommend is Parents and Friends of Ex-Gays *(www.pfox.org)*. If there is no ministry like this in your area that offers a family support group, get involved in or put together a small group of Christian friends with whom you can be honest and transparent and who will support you and pray for you as you travel down this new road.

- A word of warning: One parent group you DO NOT WANT to contact for help or support is P-FLAG (Parents and Friends of Lesbians and Gays). This group is strongly gay-affirming and, sadly, is the one regularly recommended by columnist Ann Landers as well as the United States Department of Education. This organization has affiliates in all fifty states, and schools and community agencies often refer families to them. Not only is the organization strongly pro-gay, but their literature and recommended reading lists also specifically encourage teens or young people to use only their feelings as a guide to sexual behavior, to be their own judge of what is right and wrong, and to feel free to experiment in sexual behaviors. P-FLAG views those holding traditional religious beliefs as mean-spirited and hypocritical.[2]

The Search Begins

Today, it is hard to imagine life without the Internet or searching for information without Google, but a word of caution is necessary about using the Internet as a source for information on homosexuality. One will find a wealth of information to be sure, but most of it will be from a pro-homosexual perspective, and the pro-gay arguments can be very persuasive for the person looking for answers but not yet equipped with a strong biblical understanding of this subject. The source you turn to for information is very important; make sure your source is trustworthy and biblically based, such as the ministries listed earlier in this chapter.

Since my search in 1992 was BI (Before Internet), I hesitantly made my way to a large, Christian bookstore in Miami where I often shopped for Christian books. I say hesitantly because, admittedly, I was more than a little nervous as I drove toward the bookstore. I didn't have a clue what books to look for or even if there were any books available that had been written by Christians on homosexual issues. I sure didn't feel comfortable asking one of the clerks in the store for help, and what if I should run into someone I knew? That possibility alarmed me and tempted me to turn the car around and head back home. But knew I couldn't chicken out on this important first step in my search.

At the bookstore, I walked up and down several aisles, not even knowing what category to look under, until finally, probably by divine intervention, I came to a section where I found several books on homosexuality. I scooped them up like an uncovered treasure, holding them close to my chest to make the titles as invisible as possible, and praying I would not run into someone I knew on my way to the checkout counter. How would I explain what I was doing with *these* books? When I arrived at the counter and saw that the clerk was someone unfamiliar to me, I breathed a sigh of relief and a quick "Thank you, Lord." I knew that many hours of reading lay ahead, but I found myself eager to start, hoping that in these books I would find the answers to my many questions.

In 1992, the availability of good books on the subject of homosexuality from reliable Christian sources was much more limited than it is today. But the ones I did acquire at that time proved to be God's good provision and gave me important and much-needed information and direction. In the years that followed, I continued to build my stockpile of knowledge as more books were published on the subject.

Born Gay?

Dan first informed me of his gay identity in 1992. A study conducted in 1991 by neurobiologist Simon LeVay was widely referenced and publicized as "proof" that homosexuality has a genetic origin.

The scope of LeVay's study of the brains of homosexual cadavers was very small, and the validity of his conclusions was disputed by a number of scientists. Even LeVay himself made a disclaimer that further interpretations of the results of his study needed to be considered speculative. Of course, the initial claims announced by LeVay (who was gay) were widely publicized and accepted as "proof" that homosexuality was inborn while his disclaimer and subsequent concerns about the study expressed by the scientific community were virtually ignored. In addition, the results of LeVay's study were never duplicated by other studies. LeVay later stated:

> I did not prove that homosexuality is genetic, or find a genetic cause for being gay. I did not show that gay men are born that way, the most common mistake people make in interpreting my work.[3]

When these statements of LeVay were published later, they were largely disregarded. The damage was already done. Like feathers scattered in the wind, the biased and inaccurate conclusions of the study had rapidly spread and were quickly embraced and promoted primarily by the gay community and the media as facts.

In 1993, geneticist Dean Hamer published a study in which he claimed to have found a gene that he theorized might be the cause for male homosexuality. The misleading media headlines loudly proclaimed, GAY GENE FOUND, and that became further evidence to support the "born gay" argument. It should be noted that Hamer was not completely unbiased in his research since he was an activist for gay causes. Later, when two other researchers tried to duplicate Hamer's results in an even larger study, they were never able to do so and expressed their concern over wide discrepancies between Hamer's study and their study. Hamer's later "clarification" that homosexuality was not rooted solely in biology largely went unnoted by the media. The original incorrect message in the sensational headlines of the press was what the public remembered.

Joseph Nicolosi, PhD, a clinical psychologist and past president and one of the founding members of the National Association for Research and Therapy of Homosexuality, writes in much more detail about these and subsequent studies in his book *A Parent's Guide to Preventing Homosexuality*. Thus, the off-repeated assumption of "born gay" was strongly planted in the minds of the public. But the more I read on the subject, the more I accepted the validity of the position of many counselors and unbiased researchers that to date no unbiased, scientific studies substantiate the "born gay" premise.

Over the years, the search for a "gay gene" has continued as many researchers have attempted to prove the theory of "born gay." Interestingly, when I began writing this book in 2009, the American Psychological Association published a brochure that updated its earlier brochure published in 1998. The earlier brochure had stated, "There is considerable recent evidence to suggest that biology, including genetic or inborn hormonal factors, play a significant role in a person's sexuality."[4] But the updated brochure, entitled, "Answers to Your Questions for a Better Understanding of Sexual Orientation & Homosexuality," includes an admission that there is no "gay gene":

> Although much research has examined the possible genetic, hormonal, developmental, social, and cultural influences on sexual orientation, no finds have emerged that permit scientists to conclude that sexual orientation is determined by any particular factor or factors. Many think that both nature and nurture play complex roles.[5]

In 1996, Dr. Jeffrey Satinover, a former fellow in psychiatry and child psychiatry at Yale University with many years of practice in psychoanalysis and psychiatry, authored a book, *Homosexuality and the Politics of Truth*, which was acclaimed by the Congressional Record to be "the best book on homosexuality written in our lifetime." Considering Dr. Satinover's reputation in this field, his statements listed below shed some necessary light and lend weight to the important question of the role of genetics in homosexual behavior:

> The real genetic question is—what is it in the background of people who become homosexual that opens the door for them, where the door is essentially closed for other people? In a nutshell, *every* behavioral trait in human nature has a genetic component. For example, basketball playing is clearly genetic . . . But if you ask yourself what that's about, it's clear that it's NOT that there is a gene for basketball playing. The reason there's a genetic association is that there's an *intermediate* trait which allows people who carry these traits to become basketball players in greater numbers than those who do *not* have those traits—namely, height, athleticism, and so on. So it's not surprising that there is a growing number of studies that show a genetic association to homosexuality. But that is a far cry from saying that homosexuality is genetic in the way that eye color is genetic.[6]

Dr. Joseph Nicolosi, quoting psychiatrist Satinover, acknowledges that there are no doubt genetic or prenatal hormonal influences that "open the door" to homosexuality for some people, and these influences may induce a child to see him- or herself as gender-atypical, but that is not to conclude that people are "born gay."[7]

Even though to date no study has ever proven conclusive, there is still the commonly held belief that homosexuality is inborn, and that belief continues to be perpetuated by widely read people like advice columnist Ann Landers and other public figures.

Same-Sex Attractions a Choice?

But if people are not born gay, homosexuality must be a choice, right? Again, my lack of understanding and information about the complexity of the homosexual condition made it easy to draw a wrong conclusion at this point. I wrongly assumed that Dan must have made a decision at some point to be gay. In the early days of my search for answers, I made a comment to Dan about "choosing" to be gay. He looked at me with an anguished expression and exclaimed, "Mother! Why would anyone 'choose' to be this way?"

His response and tone of voice showed the pain he felt over his same-sex attractions and homosexual condition, a pain I had not previously recognized but now needed to understand. But if Dan was not born gay and didn't consciously or deliberately choose to be attracted to other men, what was the source of these same-sex attractions? How did he become gay?

No Simple Answers

It didn't take me long to realize that my search for answers would not be quick or easy.

This was not going to be like a twelve-step program. There was not a concise list of "Twelve Reasons Why Your Child Is Gay," nor was there a book entitled, *Twelve Steps to Fix Your Gay Child*. I was discovering that the homosexual condition, although not proven to be caused by a "gay gene," was very complex. Elizabeth R. Moberly states in her book *Homosexuality: A New Christian Ethic*, a recognized classic on the subject, "It might be truer to say that the phenomenon of homosexuality is more complex and many-faceted than might at first sight be apparent . . . The causation of homosexuality is not a simple matter."[8]

There was not a "one size fits all" answer to why a person develops attractions for his own sex. However, what I did learn was that the many in-depth studies and the counseling of many men and women struggling with unwanted same-sex attractions seemed to reveal some common factors in many of their backgrounds. These are often referred to as the "roots" of homosexuality.

Before briefly looking at some of these common factors, I need to emphasize again the complexity of the development of human sexuality. In Dr. William Consiglio's book *Homosexual No More*, I came across two diagrams he used to illustrate his view of the development of homosexuality.

The first diagram showed what he called the stream of sexuality, showing a small child starting out in the stream of heterosexuality, with the waters of sexuality pictured as a gently flowing shallow stream about the depth of his ankles. But as the child progresses to and through adolescence, the stream of sexuality increases in depth and strength. It becomes hot (very pleasurable), rapid (very powerful), finally reaching the height of his chin (very pervasive). For the rest of adulthood, sexuality continues to be a powerful and pervasive force in a person's life.

Dr. Consiglio's second diagram again showed the stream of sexuality as a stream of heterosexuality, and he noted two important points:

- That the stream of sexuality was created by God as a heterosexual one and "has as its outlet, physical, emotional, and spiritual bonding with the opposite sex."
- That "human sexuality is a powerful force that is always flowing."

He points out that a flowing stream of water cannot be stopped. You can block it with pebbles, rocks, or boulders, but it will find a way to flow over or around those blockages and continue to flow, eventually developing into a stream with a different path.

Dr. Consiglio then states that human sexuality is like that powerful flowing stream. "It will always be active to find expression in one form or another. If the stream of human sexuality is blocked in childhood or adolescence, it will likely form other streams (deviations or disorientations) off of the mainstream . . . Homosexuality is one of the most common disorientations."[9]

In the second diagram, some of the "pebbles and rocks" that can block and eventually divert the stream of heterosexuality are identified as unresolved family/parental relationships, lack of good peer relationships, ineffective techniques for dealing with temptation, lack of understanding about homosexuality, and others. Some of the boulders are low self-esteem, gender emptiness, wounded area of emotions, sexual abuse, negative interior conversations, and spiritual devitalization.[10]

This visual presentation was a big help to me as I read about some of the factors that can influence a person to develop same-sex attractions and participate in homosexual activity. I began to identify some of those pebbles, rocks, and boulders in my son's life and how his sexual development had been negatively influenced by them.

Joe Dallas also emphasized the importance of not overlooking the complexity of the homosexual condition when looking for answers to "How can my child be gay?" He makes this point in *Desires in Conflict,* one of several excellent books he has written on the subject of homosexuality:

> My objection to all these theories [of origin of same-sex attractions] is that they assume each person has homosexual conditions for the same reason. I would argue that, like other problems, its roots vary from individual to individual . . . We've got to approach this subject with a respect for the complexity of human sexuality in general.[11]

It must also be noted that one or more of the common factors may be present in a person's life, but they do not automatically trigger the development of same-sex attractions. Having said that, I want to share a few of the common factors that seem more prevalent in the lives of homosexuals and lesbians and that were particularly helpful in understanding my son.

Chapter 6

Some Answers Emerge

Gender Identity

One very important piece of information I learned was that a predominant factor in the development of same-sex attractions is confusion about gender identity. In his book *A Parent's Guide to Preventing Homosexuality,* Joseph Nicolosi states, "At the very heart of the homosexual condition is a conflict about gender. In the boy, we usually see a gender wound that dates back to childhood. He comes to see himself different from other boys."[1] And in their book *Unwanted Harvest,* Mona Riley and Brad Sargent give this description for gender identity:

> It is the heart-level alliance one feels (or does not feel) with his or her God-given gender. Boys should grow up feeling masculine—that they fit in with other boys and men. Girls should grow up feeling feminine—that they fit in with other girls and women. However sometimes these internal allegiances get crossed, especially for those who end up with homosexual feelings: Boys often feel more allied with women, femininity, and women's culturally defined roles; girls often feel more allied with men, masculinity, and men's culturally defined roles. They do not identify with their God-ordained gender.[2]

Julie Hamilton, PhD, is a licensed marriage and family therapist, an assistant professor of psychology at Palm Beach Atlantic University, and former president of the National Association of Research and Therapy of Homosexuality (NARTH). In 2006, Dr. Hamilton produced a very informative CD, *Homosexuality 101*, which gives an overview of how gender identity is formed in a person's life. I found this very important and helpful and, with Dr. Hamilton's permission, I want to share a summary of some of her information.

I need to say first that Dr. Hamilton's presentation on development of gender identity is primarily from the male perspective, which is easier to understand because, she states, the female development is a little more complex. I will look at the development of lesbianism in the next chapter.

Normal Development of Gender Identity (Male)

- When babies are born, they initially see themselves as one with their mother, but eventually they are able to see themselves as a separate entity.
- Around the age of eighteen months, babies are beginning to be able to recognize the difference between genders—Daddy is a boy, Mommy is a girl.
- About the age of two and a half, the toddler boy must be able to begin to separate himself from his attachment to his mother and attach himself to his father. The relationship between a boy and his father is the initial source of a secure gender identity. From the years of two and a half to four, the little boy starts to develop a sense of who he is as a male, including who he is as a little boy and how little boys act. It is through the father-son relationship between a boy and his father that a boy discovers what he needs to know about being male. Unconsciously, he is looking to his father to give him worth and value as a little boy. The father does this by spending time

with his small son, showing interest in his son—especially in the things his son is interested in and giving verbal and physical affirmation of his love and acceptance. Dr. Hamilton points out that it is actually through playful touch that a little boy develops a sense of his own masculine body.

- At the age of five or six, a little boy reaches another stage of development, a time when he begins to attach to his peers. This is the age that children normally begin school, so he now looks to other boys his age to discover how they walk, talk, and play and how he measures up in relationship to them. He seeks to be accepted by them, to bond with them and be affirmed as a boy. For the next several years, he needs to spend time bonding with his same sex. During these years, little boys usually do not want to spend time with the opposite sex. Girls are "icky" and are not allowed into boys' clubhouses! Dr. Hamilton states that this is a God-given stage of development. Persons need to understand and bond with members of their own sex before they can become interested in and bond with members of the opposite sex. A boy needs that steady connecting or bonding with his own sex from the young age of two to three years old all the way up to puberty to give him the strong sense of who he is as a male before he can be attracted to the opposite sex. Then when he reaches puberty, he can begin to wonder what girls are all about. Girls become what Dr. Hamilton describes as the "intriguing and mysterious gender." His curiosity becomes a sexual interest and a desire for romantic connection with the opposite sex.

But what if there is not this normal development of a strong identity with a person's God-created gender? And how can this factor into the development of same-sex attractions instead of attractions to the opposite sex? Dr. Hamilton states that for the child who will develop a homosexual orientation, the process of normal development of gender identity does not happen.

A common misconception is that homosexual men fall into easily identified appearances or behaviors. A friend of mine, who had seen my son with me when he occasionally came to church functions before I disclosed he was gay, once made the statement in my hearing, "I can always spot a gay person." I couldn't help but chuckle inwardly because I knew she didn't have a clue my son was gay-identified. Later, when I publicly shared this information about my son, I could tell she was caught completely off-guard. Dr. Joseph Nicolosi, PhD, in his book *Reparative Therapy of Male Homosexuality*, makes this interesting statement:

> Male gender-identity deficit does not mean simply that this man fails to fit into his culture's image of masculinity. The heterosexual may have an artistic nature and enjoy theater, art, and cooking; on the other hand, the homosexual may be a rodeo rider or professional football player. Rather, it refers to an inadequacy in the inner sense of maleness or femaleness. Gender-identity deficit is the internal, private sense of incompleteness or inadequacy about one's maleness, and this is not always evident in explicit effeminate traits. Some outwardly masculine homosexual men have carefully cultivated their outer images as an armor against inner anxieties of masculine inadequacy.[3]

Interruptions in the Normal Development of Gender Identity

Typically, for the boy who does not develop a strong sense of his gender, there is something that prevents him from attaching to his father. Bob Davies and Lori Rentzel, in their book *Coming Out of Homosexuality*, point out that young boys who lose their father through traumatic events like death or divorce can be left yearning for love and protection from a man. They also state that sexual identity seems to be more noticeably shaped by disrupted bonding with the same-sex parent, i.e., little girls lacking an intimate attachment to Mom and boys feeling detached and alienated from Dad.[4]

Elizabeth R. Moberly also stresses the potential damage that can come from disrupted bonding:

> Any incident that disrupts the child's attachment to the parent of the same sex may result in the homosexual condition, but it may be most clearly illustrated in the case of early separation. Such separation, even if relatively brief, may lead to a typical process of mourning; protest at the absence of the loved parent, followed by despair, leading finally to detachment. When the child is reunited with the parent, it may take some time for normal attachment to be restored, since the child has experienced the parent as being hurtful ("he/she abandoned me") even if the separation was unavoidable and there was no intention of hurt.[5]

The importance of the relationship and bonding between a father and his son cannot be overstated. Joseph Nicolosi, in his excellent book *A Parent's Guide to Preventing Homosexuality*, states:

> In fifteen years, I have spoken with hundreds of homosexual men. Perhaps there are exceptions, but I have never met a single homosexual man who said he had a close, loving, and respectful relationship with his father . . . In our own clinical work, and from the experience of the many men we have known, it seems very rare for a man who struggles with homosexuality to feel that he was sufficiently loved, affirmed, and mentored by his father while growing up or to feel that he identified with his father as a male role model.[6]

In Dr. Nicolosi's discussion of "Gender Identify Is Established Within the Context of a Family," he states very plainly, "The father plays a pivotal role in a boy's normal development as a male. The truth is, Dad is more important to the boy's gender identity development than is Mom."[7]

Failure of a young boy to attach and bond with the father may be caused in a number of ways:

- He may not have a father or a father figure in his life because of death, divorce, or being raised by a single mother or other women.
- His father may be in the home but gone much of the time because of work responsibilities or involvement in other activities so there is no time to spend with his small son.
- The father may be physically present and a "nice guy" but emotionally absent and detached from his son, unable to give emotionally of himself to his young son and leaving the parenting entirely to the mother.
- There may be a temperamental mismatch. The father may find it hard to relate to his son's sensitive temperament and may not share common interests with his son. For example, the father may be strongly interested in sports and rugged outdoor activities and cannot understand or relate to his son's interests, which are more social, artistic, and less typically masculine.
- The father may love his son but have a strong, overbearing, or explosive personality, which may make him seem threatening and unsafe to a very young child.
- A father may unavoidably be away from the home frequently or for long durations in the very early years of a young boy's life because of military deployments, a job that requires extended travel, or other extenuating circumstances that remove the father from the home and from his child's life during those crucial, formative stages.
- A father may be verbally or even physically abusive to his small son, calling him names, i.e., dumb, stupid, clumsy, or

administering harsh physical treatment for minor infractions, causing his son to fear his father and put up protective barriers against the father in his mind, emotions, and interactions with him.

The above factors, though some may be unavoidable, can still disrupt the normal and essential bonding process between the small son and his father and can even be perceived by a small child as abandonment by his father.

It is also important to know that in the case of an absent father other strong males, such as a loving and caring grandfather or a brother who is several years older, may fill the vital role of a father figure in the young child's life by spending time with him and providing a strong, male influence.

As Dr. Hamilton points out in her paper, "Homosexuality 101: What Every Therapist, Parent, and Homosexual Should Know," it is important to note that:

> There are many children who grow up without fathers and yet do not develop a homosexual orientation. In addition, there are many children who have loving fathers, yet still become homosexually oriented. This is due to the fact that various factors can contribute to a homosexual orientation. Human development is very complex and includes events, as well as perceptions about events.[8]

Perception can play a very important role in the development of gender identity. It's not so much what really happened in the home or the parent-child relationship but how the child *perceived* the event and relationship. The child's perception becomes his reality. If he perceives that his father does not love him or the father's absence from the home or lack of attention to him as abandonment, he will emotionally respond out of that perception. Joe Dallas states that *perception* and *response* are the key words in the situation:

> In all relationships, we perceive the other party as having a certain attitude toward us, and we respond to the other party according to our own perception of that attitude . . . Likewise, a child may have had parents who loved and highly valued him, but for some reason the communication of that love got blurred. He may have perceived his father to be disinterested when, in fact, the father cared very much . . . In both cases, whether the child experienced *actual* rejection from the parent of the same sex, or whether he simply *perceived* that rejection, he will have responded emotionally. And that emotional response is, in many cases, the beginning of strong, unfulfilled needs, contributing to homosexual attractions.[9]

This negative impact of a child's early perception of rejection or indifference from the same gender parent is often seen in adults who develop homosexual attractions.

A child's perception of events and relationships is also influenced by his temperament. While a child is not born gay, the biological factor of his temperament does influence his perception and how experiences may impact him. Boys who are born with a sensitive, intuitive, or artistic temperament can be more vulnerable to the negative impact of disruptions in their relationships with their fathers and to other wounding experiences of life.

Dr. Hamilton addresses the role of temperament in this way: "Typically the child who will later develop same-sex attractions is naturally sensitive, observant, intelligent, creative, and sometimes more artistic than athletic. This child often tends to personalize and internalize experiences and observations."[10]

If a young child perceives that his father does not want a relationship with him and has rejected him, the boy may choose to reject his father in return. Usually, the child at this point will stay connected to the mother and begins to develop a sense of the feminine instead of understanding his own maleness.

Childhood and School Years

By the time a child enters school, he may already be having difficulty relating to other boys. He feels more comfortable with girls and relates more easily to them. He feels "different" from other boys and often feels intimidated by them and inadequate to participate in their boy activities. At the same time, he craves acceptance by the other boys, but because he tends to associate more with girls as friends and participate in their activities, other boys may tease and ridicule him, even calling him names, such as "sissy" or "girl." This rejection and ridicule of other boys further wounds his sensitive spirit and often causes him to withdraw even more. He desires to understand himself in terms of his own masculine identity; yet he is not able to integrate with his same-sex parent or same-sex peers, so he does not acquire a masculine identity or develop a secure gender identity.

Even a young boy's body build can negatively affect how he perceives himself and how others react to him. If he is substantially overweight for his age but still active in the physical activities of other boys, he is often teased and ridiculed with names like "fatso," "blimp," "tubby," or worse. If a young boy has little or no interest in sports but would rather be involved in the arts or academics and is teased and labeled with belittling nicknames, his feeling of being different from other boys may be amplified and cause him to withdraw and pursue solitary pursuits or find acceptance in the familiar company of girls his age. None of these factors in and of themselves cause development of homosexual orientation, but they can contribute to feelings of alienation from same-sex peers and his sense of low esteem.

Dr. Hamilton further explains that by the time the young boy reaches puberty, the craving for male input has grown and intensified. Unlike his male peers, he is not interested in the opposite sex, because he already knows all about them. What he craves to know about is his own gender. He longs to experience connection with males.

Unmet Emotional Needs

When approaching adolescence, the child who has not had a healthy relationship with the same-sex parent and has a severe deficit in same-sex bonding may continue to seek this missing intimacy. Thus, instead of connecting and bonding with the opposite sex, he finds himself left behind while his peers go forward. Not only does this increase the sense of alienation he already feels, it also intensifies his deep need for emotionally satisfying friendships with those of the same sex.

Joe Dallas points out that strong emotional needs can become sexualized, linking with sexual desires. The object of the emotional need also becomes the object of the sexual desire.[11] During puberty, the normal developing and strengthening sex drive can collide with deep-rooted, unmet, same-sex emotional needs, and they become homosexual desires.

It is important to remember that the deep emotional need for acceptance, affection, and affirmation from the same sex is a normal, healthy, and legitimate need. But, as pointed out earlier, sometimes these needs are not met. Joe Dallas further states, "This, to my thinking, is how it often begins: A normal yet unmet need for bonding with a member of the same sex remains unsatisfied, leaving the boy or girl yearning for, then seeking out, fulfillment of these normal needs through abnormal behaviors such as homosexuality."[12]

Others in the field of counseling ministries to homosexuals agree. Mona Riley and Brad Sargent write, "The unmet legitimate desire for same-sex relational intimacy (i.e., a strong, safe, and normal friendship) becomes an illegitimate desire for sexual intimacy. Some are able to say no to homosexual involvement. Many do not, and feelings turn into actions."[13]

My good friend Christine Sneeringer, at the time of this writing the director of Worthy Creations in Fort Lauderdale, Florida, a ministry to those struggling with same-sex attractions, has been walking in freedom from lesbianism since 1990. She is a frequent speaker at conferences, churches, and youth events. In her talks, she often makes this interesting statement, "Even though the word *sex* appears in the middle of the word, homosexuality is not really about sex; it is about relationships and unmet emotional needs."

While that statement may sound strange at first, authors Mona Riley and Brad Sargent agree with that conclusion. They state, "It would seem that a homosexual orientation is based on emotional and relational problems."[14]

Michael Saia, a Christian counselor who has ministered to the homosexual community and counseled many Christians coming from a homosexual background, shares this very interesting and corroborating experience in his book *Counseling the Homosexual*:

> "What were you looking for when you had your first homosexual experience?" I have asked many gay men this question and have received many and varied responses. But there is one answer I have never heard: "sex." Each was seeking affection, companionship, communication, identity, or security—but never sex. This curious silence made me wonder about the relationship of sex to human needs in the homosexual's life.

He subsequently concludes, "Most homosexually oriented men do not enter into relationships with other men just to have sex. Rather they are trying to fulfill their needs for unconditional love and a sense of identity."[15]

Dr. Bill Consiglio, who has extensive experience in counseling those struggling with homosexuality, states ten facts about homosexuality in his book *Homosexual No More*. Fact number seven is:

> Homosexuality has very little to do with sex. It has much more to do with an emotional and psychological wound which leaves a person feeling deprived, empty, unfulfilled, and incomplete in the bonding that he needed

to experience with the same gender parent . . . The sexual aspect of homosexuality is an attempt to meet the love and intimacy needs which were never adequately formed between the child and the same-sex parent.[16]

Time and time again, as I continued to read the writings and conclusions of those who were well-qualified to speak to the issue of homosexuality, I was reminded of the complexity of human sexuality, of the *many* factors that can *contribute* to development of a homosexual orientation in a person, and that the same exact set of factors is not seen in every homosexual. Thus, while it may not be said with certainty what precisely causes the development of homosexual orientation in each individual, it is evident that many of the same factors are seen with frequency in those with homosexual attractions. While there may be some inborn predispositions, such as a sensitive temperament, that may make a person more vulnerable to homosexuality or a biological predisposition, those alone are not sufficient in and of themselves to produce same-sex attractions. However, as Dr. Consiglio points out, what is commonly seen in the lives of homosexuals are other environmental or developmental factors, such as the unhealthy behavior or relationship of the same-sex parent, emotional rejection, dysfunctional family relationships, sexual abuse, emotional and/or physical abuse, disappointing relationships with peers, and even medical handicaps or problems that isolate a young child or adolescent from their peers.[17] It is understandable how a combination of some of these factors in a young child's life can produce a poor self-image and low self-esteem.

As I share my journey and experiences in this book, I am not attempting to be exhaustive in communicating all the information on homosexuality that I found in those early days or that is even more abundant and available today. There are many excellent resources from those I would classify as experts that can provide more expansive and in-depth treatment of this issue, and I encourage others to avail themselves of these. (Some of these resources are listed at the back of this book.) Understandably, my initial pursuit of answers to the question, "How could my son be gay?" was very personal, and I viewed my accumulating information through the filter of how did this apply to my son. Later, when the Lord provided opportunities to minister to other parents of gay children, my interest and research broadened to how I might help other parents as well.

Chapter 7

The Damaging Role of Sexual Abuse

My Son's Story

I am very aware that Dan has placed great trust in me by giving me permission to write our story. I say "our" because this is not just the record of my journey and my struggles and growth as a parent. It is very much his story too, and as I write this section, I want to respect not only his trust, but his privacy as well.

Dan was about twenty years old when I first learned that the son of one of my close friends had been sexually abused when he was a young adolescent by a man we both knew and trusted. We later discovered that her son was not his only victim, and that raised concern and questions in my mind as to whether he might have also abused my son. The perpetrator had been a close friend of our family, even living with us for several months at one point many years earlier. Over the years, my husband, Jerry, had tried to fill the vacuum of both father and big brother relationships in the life of this young man.

When Jerry died, Dan was just six weeks shy of his thirteenth birthday. Since I had no reason not to trust this supposed "friend" of our family, I allowed Dan to spend a good amount of time with him at that time. Years later, when the abuse situation came to light, I knew I needed to question Dan.

By this time, he was no longer living at home, but one day when the opportunity presented itself, I asked him if anyone had ever approached or touched him inappropriately. Dan responded, "No." I pressed him further. "And you would tell me if this had happened to you?" Dan's answer was yes, so I dropped the matter.

A few years later, when more evidence of the extent of sexual abuse by the same man began to surface, I knew I needed to approach Dan again about the possibility that he had been victimized. Thus it came about on that same Easter Sunday in 1992, before I could voice my questions about the abuse, Dan had hesitantly and tearfully made his painful disclosure that he was gay. The revelation of his gay identity made my question much easier to ask, and this time, Dan readily admitted he had been involved sexually with this man. He told me he knew whom I was referring to when I had questioned him previously, but that he had lied to me. A forceful statement quickly followed his admission. "Don't ask me to testify against Ben, Mom. I won't do it! It was my fault too."

Although at that time I knew very little about sexual abuse, I knew enough to be able to respond strongly but reassuringly. "Son, it's never the fault of a young boy when he is sexually abused by an older male. It's always totally the fault and wrong actions of the older person. Ben was the one who took advantage of you. You cannot blame yourself for any of it."

Later, I would learn that young victims of abuse often feel that they are responsible for what happened to them, and they struggle for years with feelings of self-blame—that somehow they caused the abuse. This assumption by the victim, plus the overwhelming sense of shame, frequently causes him or her to shrink back from being publicly involved in bringing the perpetrator to justice. As Dan and I continued to talk on that Easter Sunday afternoon, I kept using the words *sexually abused* and *molested* until Dan interjected, "I wasn't abused." But I quickly corrected him. "You can call it what you want, son, but you *were* abused. When an older adult takes advantage of a child or adolescent and initiates a sexual relationship with him, it is sexual abuse." At that time, I was perplexed about the sense of loyalty Dan seemed to have toward this man. But later, as I learned more about the confusion that sexual abuse creates in the minds and hearts of young victims, it became more understandable.

Molesters hold powerful emotional control over their young victims. In the vast majority of cases, the offender is someone the child knows and loves—and therefore trusts. In my son's case, this was certainly true. His abuser had lived in our home for a number of months when my son was about seven years old and had been in and out of his life during the subsequent years. As I stated earlier, this young man was a close friend of Dan's father. There was no reason to view him with anything but trust and friendship. Interestingly, Davies and Rentzel state, "Offenders have an uncanny ability to target children who are lonely . . . or needing attention . . ."[1]

When I questioned my son about when the abuse had started, he informed me it was the summer after his father had died. Even as I write this, many years later, the strong emotion of justified anger toward this man who so wrongly took advantage of my young son threatens to reemerge, though I thought I had dealt with it. At the age of thirteen, Dan was just coming into puberty, a time when he would normally be dealing with the emergence of his developing sexuality. He was extremely emotionally vulnerable as he struggled with the loss and absence of his father and was experiencing a normal craving for the love and security of a father, a father now lost to him forever in this life. At this young age, he would not have been able to identify or verbalize these deep emotional needs, but their presence created a gaping vacuum and made him an easy prey for his perpetrator to draw into a sexual relationship, resulting in enormous confusion and emotional damage to my son.

Not only was the sexual abuse a massive violation of trust by the perpetrator, it was also extremely confusing and damaging to my son's concept of God and the validity of Christianity. This man was a professing Christian, quick to share his views on the Bible and his relationship with God, while behind closed doors he was sexually abusing my son and other young boys. Sadly, my son is not the only one who has been subjected to abuse by a trusted Christian leader, such as a youth pastor, deacon, Sunday school teacher, or camp counselor. This source of sexual abuse brings a whole new spiritual dimension to the damage from sexual abuse.

A few years later, when my son was going through a very difficult breakup with his second partner, I became very concerned about his emotional well-being and strongly encouraged him to consider counseling. He agreed to see a counselor, someone on his insurance plan at work, but I stressed to him the importance of seeing a Christian counselor. I explained that God created us as triune beings—body, soul, and spirit—and that a secular counselor would only see him as a soul and body and would not address, or even acknowledge, the important spiritual dimension. A Christian counselor would rightly address all three aspects of his person. Thankfully, Dan saw the wisdom of this argument and agreed to see a Christian therapist I knew who specialized in sexual problems. When Dan asked me to make an appointment for him, I stressed that he needed to talk to the counselor about the sexual abuse, and he promised he would.

Obviously, I was very thankful to the Lord that Dan agreed to see the therapist, and I prayed he would bond with the counselor and feel comfortable talking with him not only about his present emotional struggles but about the sexual abuse as well. I knew Dan was nervous about his first visit, but out of respect for Dan's privacy and the importance of the confidentiality of the sessions, I did not plan to ask him any questions about how the first session had gone. However, to my surprise, Dan told me he liked the counselor and thought they got off to a good start. I chuckled to myself when he told me how the first session began. After Dan sat down in the counselor's office, his first words were very direct. "I'm gay. Is that a problem for you?"

The counselor's response was just as direct. "Not at all. I have a number of clients who are homosexuals, but you need to know I counsel from a biblical perspective. Is that a problem for you?"

Dan responded, "No, not a problem," and they were off to a good, honest start.

After several visits with the counselor, one night Dan unexpectedly said to me, "Did you know I could still bring charges against Ben if I wanted to?"

"Yes, I know you could, and I would support you if you decided to do that."

Dan didn't pursue the matter any further that night, but I knew he had made a major breakthrough regarding the sexual abuse. He no longer blamed himself, and the erroneous and misplaced sense of loyalty toward his abuser had been shattered. Even though Dan discontinued the sessions after a few months, I believe they served a useful purpose in helping him to face more realistically the abuse in his past and see it for what it was. I saw it as a very important first step in his dealing with the experience.

Sexual Abuse—A Contributing Factor

Sexual abuse is recognized as one of the possible and frequently appearing factors in the development of same-sex attractions and ensuing homosexual behavior. This painful and shame-filled experience in the life of a child or adolescent often stays hidden from others as a dark and troubling part of his or her past. It is important to bring this issue into the light because of its great potential for extensive harm to the victim. Additionally, I believe it played a significant role in my son's concluding that he was gay and his subsequent involvement in homosexual behavior.

It has been discovered that sexual abuse is one of the most common and most damaging denominators found in both male and female homosexuals. Does this mean that all homosexuals, gay or lesbian, have been abused sometime during their childhood or teenage years? No, but sadly, sexual abuse (including molestation and rape) has been found to be a key factor in homosexuality. Studies indicate that many male homosexuals have been abused as children or adolescents and many others were physically or emotionally abused.

For lesbians, sexual abuse is one of the primary factors that result in their embracing lesbianism. Anita Worthan writes in her book *Someone I Love Is Gay,* that several Exodus leaders have estimated 80 to 90 percent of the women coming for help to ex-gay ministries have been victims of sexual abuse.[2] Most often, the abuser is a trusted friend, a male family member, or, even more tragically, the father of the female victim.

When an older male molests or draws a young boy, particularly an adolescent, into a sexual relationship, one of the harmful effects on the adolescent is confusion about his sexual identity. It raises questions in his mind: Why was the older man attracted to him sexually? He was the sexual partner of a man. Does that make him a woman? A homosexual? Bob Davies and Lori Rentzel point out in their book *Coming Out of Homosexuality* that the abused "boy may grow up feeling vulnerable, weak, and defenseless. He feels detached from his own masculinity—the exact dynamic that leads to a search for this male identity through sexual experiences with other boys or men. One researcher found that young males sexually abused by older males were about four times more likely to engage in homosexual activity as adults than non-victimized males."[3]

Anita Worthen points out, "Typically, boys who are abused *repeatedly* by a perpetrator experience some physical pleasure and may seek to repeat the acts with other boys in order to duplicate the feelings of sexual pleasure and physical closeness" (emphasis added).[4] If a young boy is repeatedly molested by an older man and discovers his body responds with physical pleasure to the stimulation of his sexual organs or the actual sexual act, he may understandably but erroneously assume he must be gay or he would not be experiencing pleasure in that situation. At that young age, he does not have the knowledge or understanding to recognize that the human body was designed by God to respond to stimulation of the genital organs with a sense of pleasure, even when the circumstances of that stimulation are wrong and perverted. Don Schmierer, in his book *An Ounce of Prevention,* makes the statement, "Sometimes young men who have been molested develop a homosexual condition because they have learned to function sexually in that way through molestation."[5]

Joe Dallas describes the destructive impact of sexual abuse this way:

> Sexual violation is a peculiar evil that has left many a boy or girl desolate. The effects of it can be guessed at but never really measured. It is, among all crimes, one of the most sinister and devastating. And often, the devastation shows itself in sexual confusion.[6]

The old adage that "time heals all wounds" does not apply to the victims of sexual abuse. The damage done cannot be ignored or dismissed lightly. Sadly, the lives of abuse survivors have been scarred forever by the sins of their perpetrator(s).

Joe Dallas also states that the contributing factor of sexual abuse to homosexuality is manifested differently in men and women. A girl who has been sexually abused often concludes that men are unsafe, that men view women only as sex objects to satisfy their sexual lusts. Understandably, this view of men as being unsafe prevents any future bonding with a male partner. But surprisingly, a boy who has been sexually abused may find that the experience actually binds him to other males as sexual partners instead of just friends or pals.[7]

For women, the trauma of sexual abuse often results in the development of anger, rage, and hatred directed at all men. If the abuser is a member of the young girl's family—a brother, uncle, cousin, and especially if it is her father—the damage is even more devastating because these are men she would normally have trusted. These are men whom she expected to look out for her best interests, who should have been her protectors, not her perpetrators. This deep violation of trust can cause severe emotional damage and make it very difficult, if not impossible, for her to trust men or view them as a safe place. Many women who have been victimized sexually become lesbians because they view a relationship with another woman as the only alternative for a gentle, loving, sexual relationship.

Sometimes women who have been sexually abused by men deliberately try to make themselves physically unattractive or sexually unappealing to men. Their past experiences tell them men cannot be trusted, and if a man is attracted to them, it could open the door to future abuse. They feel uncomfortable in clothes that might show off their female figure so they may dress in more masculine clothes, even wearing men's clothing. Some may go so far as to gain a lot of weight to minimize any sexual appeal to men since they believe any sexual appeal would be a threat to their security.[8]

I have only given a brief overview of the damaging effects of sexual abuse on men and women in their childhood or adolescence and have drawn heavily on published works of those qualified to write on this issue, seeking to give proper acknowledgment when drawing from those sources. For readers interested in more in-depth study, Dr. Dan Allender, PhD, gives an excellent treatment of the damaging effects of sexual abuse in his book *The Wounded Heart*.

Joe Dallas gives some very wise and important counsel to families as they consider the impact of sexual abuse on the development of homosexuality:

> This theory *(sexual abuse a contributing factor)* opens the possibility that someone you love was violated. But you should by no means assume the possibility is a fact, unless you have objective proof of your loved one's firsthand testimony. So please don't jump to the conclusion . . . that he or she is a survivor. Remember, no one theory fits all cases. If then, your family member has not indicated such a thing, and you have no evidence it ever happened, then assume there are other reasons for the homosexuality . . . The bottom line? In many cases, early sexual violation plays a role in adult homosexuality. And although it should never be taken for granted that an adult homosexual was molested, it can be, and often is, the case. So if, in your family discussions, you learn that your

gay loved one was violated, refer him or her to a licensed Christian mental-health provider immediately. No matter where your loved one stands on homosexuality—whether embracing or rejecting it—he or she needs to deal with the emotional after-effects of the abuse. Do all within your power to encourage this (emphasis added).[9]

Chapter 8

The Lesbian Factors

Understandably, the early days of my search for answers focused on the development of male homosexuality without much attention to the female, or lesbian, homosexual. However, when I began to meet other parents who were also struggling with the issue of homosexuality in their families but with a daughter not a son, I knew I needed to know more about the roots of lesbianism. Were they different than the roots of homosexuality for the male?

My first opportunity came at a conference in Florida where a workshop was offered, "The Roots of Lesbianism," taught by Christine Sneeringer. I learned Christine was well-qualified to speak to this topic, as she had struggled with same-sex attractions and even lived in lesbian relationships for more than six years until she found freedom and healing through a relationship with Jesus Christ. My attendance at the workshop not only provided helpful information but also proved to be God's orchestration of a divine appointment for me to meet and develop a treasured friendship with Christine and later to serve with her in ministry.

I learned there are some shared roots of homosexuality in the male and female, as development of a homosexual orientation in a girl in some ways parallels that in a boy. One shared root is explained by Elizabeth Moberly in her book *Homosexuality, A New Christian Ethic*:

> From amidst a welter of details, one constant underlying
> principle suggests itself: that the homosexual—whether

man or woman—has suffered from some deficit in the relationship with the parent of the same sex; and that there is a corresponding drive to make good this deficit— through the medium of same-sex, or "homosexual" relationships. The primary cause of homosexuality is not an absent same-sex parent, but the child's defensive detachment toward him or her.[1]

This view is also shared by Bob Davies and Lori Rentzel, who write:

While a breakdown in the relation with the mother deeply affects both male and female babies, sexual identity seems to be more noticeably shaped by disrupted bonding with the same-sex parent. Little girls lacking an intimate attachment to Mom, boys feeling detached and alienated from Dad.[2]

Struggling with their gender identity is also a shared root, although the factors contributing to that struggle may differ somewhat. Dr. Nicolosi states the major conflict at the root of lesbianism is the girl's unconscious rejection of her female identity. "Women who become lesbians usually decide on an unconscious level that being female is undesirable or unsafe."[3]

A number of experiences in the girl's life could bring her to this conclusion:

- She may have been molested early in life by a male.
- The father may have been domineering, verbally or physically abusive, someone to be feared, not her protector whom she could trust.
- She may have viewed her mother as having a timid, passive, and extremely introverted personality and a victim of her circumstances.
- Her mother may have been narcissistic and controlling, forcing her daughter into a rigid behavior, resulting in the

daughter having a negative object of feminine identification in her mother, not someone she wanted to model.

A young girl may conclude that women are weak and easily taken advantage of and determine that she is not going to be that way. For her, being a woman symbolizes weakness. With an early negative view of men, she may conclude she does not need or want a man in her life. She may begin to admire women who are strong or masculine.

Other factors playing a part in a girl's early development may be inborn temperament or even her body build. She does not fit the normal expectations for a little girl—soft, sweet, accommodating, and loving dolls and frilly clothes. Instead, she may be very physically active, even rough and aggressive, preferring to play the more physical activities with little boys—football, wrestling, climbing trees. How the parents respond to this atypical little girl can have a profound affect on how she views her true gender identity:

> If the girl's parents are also aggressive and athletic, or at least enjoy these characteristics, she probably will grow into a strong, confident heterosexual woman. But sometimes a mother will struggle to accept an aggressive, active daughter, and the little girl will sense her mother's ambivalence. Feeling wounded and rejected, the girl may further detach from her mother, cutting herself off from the source of love she needs to help her grow into her own female identity. In turn, she is left with a same-sex love deficit, leaving her vulnerable to future lesbian involvement.[4]

A family dynamic that can also influence a young girl away from her feminine identity is when one or both parents were strongly hoping their expected child would be a boy but instead the new arrival was a girl. If the little girl early senses the disappointment from her parents that she is not the son they were hoping for, she may try to fill that role by becoming very tomboyish, dressing like a boy, and adopting the mannerisms of a boy.

As she grows older and other girls are concerned about being "pretty," having the right clothes, experimenting with make-up, and starting to like boys, she finds she does not share these interests but prefers sports and being buddies with the boys. She begins to feel more and more disconnected from other girls.

If a young girl, particularly as an adolescent or teenager, is considered physically unattractive by her classmates, not having what others would describe as natural beauty, or if she has a weight problem and feels she does not measure up to the physical standards of her peers, she can begin to struggle with her sexuality. Other unavoidable or undesirable physical difficulties, such as a hearing or speech impediment, physical deformities, or distracting skin conditions, can make a young girl believe she is different or unacceptable to her peers and feel like an outsider or outcast, leading to social ostracism. Children who experience ongoing rejection by their same-sex peers can develop a very low self-image, feeling they are not normal or that something is wrong with them.[5]

Another contributing factor mentioned by Don Schmierer, author of *An Ounce of Prevention: Preventing the Homosexual Condition*, is hormonal imbalance. A hormonal imbalance can greatly exaggerate the possibility of gender confusion in both boys and girls, "When boys are chemically inclined to appear to be unusually feminine or when girls seem unduly masculine."[6] While hormonal imbalances are medically treatable, this possibility is too often not considered by parents and other concerned adults. The problems associated with hormonal imbalance for young boys and girls "usually generates teasing, mocking, and harassment" from their peers and increases their sense of isolation.[7]

Schmierer describes the pattern of homosexual development in three stages. He defines the *homosexual orientation*, for both male and female, as a

> Set of deficits—physical, emotional and environmental—
> that set the stage for the *homosexual condition*.

> The homosexual condition may involve acting out, experimentation and eventually some level of involvement in the *homosexual lifestyle*, sometimes described as "gay" or "gay lifestyle" . . . These deficits may have manifested themselves very early in a child's life.[8]

The decade after high school is often the time when the development of lesbian or homosexual identity comes to the forefront.

> For young adults, going to college or becoming involved in the working world opens up a variety of avenues for self-expression. If a woman has any inclination toward lesbian feelings, now is the time she is likely to "go for it." . . . College roommates, feminist groups, women's athletics, the drama department, campus Christian ministries, you name it—women may find their first lover in all these places.[9]

For those already struggling with their sexual identity, their first lesbian relationship may feel wonderfully normal, like they were finally getting what they needed, while being with a man had felt strange and uncomfortable.

A history of sexual abuse is another shared contributing factor for both male and female homosexuals. Since I have already addressed this strong and injurious contributing factor to the development of homosexuality as it applies to both male and female, I will not give it much treatment in this chapter. However, it is worth noting and emphasizing the forceful assertion relating to lesbianism from the authors of *Coming Out of Homosexuality*: "While family dynamics, temperament and peer pressure strongly shape a person's sexual identity, the *single factor* that most powerfully propels a girl toward a lesbian identity is sexual abuse: incest, rape, or molestation" (emphasis added).[10]

Sexual abuse is defined by Davies and Rentzel as "any kind of sexual interchange between a child or young person and anyone bigger, stronger, or older." They identify the spectrum of sexual abuse behavior as ranging "from a lingering stare, with or without verbal comments, to inappropriate touching, kissing, oral sex, and anal or vaginal intercourse."[11] Incest—sexual contact with a family member, relative, or regular caretaker—is the most damaging form of sexual abuse, and women are more commonly its victims. The act of incest against a child or young girl leaves unbelievable and lasting damage because the child is both violated and betrayed by a person she should have been able to trust and depend on to care for her.

While we have seen that there are some shared roots and parallels in the development of the homosexual condition in the male and female child, there are a few major differences. Michael Saia, from his many years of counseling of homosexuals, lists three of these differences:

- First, the female homosexual's sense of rejection is more often related to actual acts of rejection, whereas the male homosexual complains more frequently of the absence of the father.
- Second, female homosexuals usually exhibit more heterophobia (fear of the opposite sex) than do male homosexuals. This is almost always related to some very traumatic events in the woman's life. Often the girl was beaten or sexually molested by her father or some other male relative. In some cases, the girl felt rejected by the mother because the mother would not believe the girl when she claimed to have been molested by the father. The very person the girl expected to protect her would not help her.
- Third, I have found more female homosexuals who hate men than male homosexuals who hate women. Many male homosexuals have had good relationships with their mothers, whereas most female homosexuals complain of mistreatment by their fathers.

Saia goes on to state,

> Female homosexuals seem to have an easier time receiving
> emotional healing than their male counterparts. Perhaps
> it is easier to deal with overt acts of rejection that caused
> hurt than to completely rebuild an image which was
> absent from the person's life. Repenting of bitterness and
> resentment over concrete acts is easier than trying to relate
> to a "vacuum" in the mind that is supposed to be filled
> with the image of one's father.[12]

Another area of difference between male and female homosexuals is the stronger role that emotional attachment plays in lesbian relationships. Dr. Carol Ahrens has found in her counseling practice that for the female homosexual, sexual activity is more easily abandoned than for the male homosexual because the primary gratification in lesbian relationships with other women has been emotional, not sexual. Women are more likely to struggle with emotional dependency than men.[13] Dr. Ahrens defines emotional dependency as follows:

> A state in which a woman feels totally reliant on another
> woman for safety and functioning . . . a virtual obsession
> with another woman that leaves her hooked on her as
> surely as though she were hooked on a drug. When a
> woman is emotionally dependent, she feels as though she
> literally cannot exist without the object of her affection.[14]

Emotional dependency develops when the normal need for affection, affirmation, and reassurance in childhood has not been successfully met to the point that a person can move from a natural and normal dependency as a child into the position of healthy independence.

Unhealthy dependency in adulthood is often the consequence of early abandonment, physical or emotional, by the mother or at least the perceived abandonment on the part of the female child. For whatever reasons, there were limitations (or an unwillingness) in the mother's ability to provide or communicate to her daughter a sense of being cherished and secure.[15]

Women whose need for mothering has remained unfulfilled may fall into dependent relationships without understanding what's really happening to them:

> They can go for years without closeness, then suddenly they meet someone who taps into their deepest longings. It begins innocently enough, appearing to be nothing more than a nice friendship. Gradually, though, the friendship becomes a snare. Both parties become more reliant on the relationship, giving it priority over everything else . . . They've finally met somebody who makes them feel wonderfully loved, totally satisfied . . . Is it any wonder that their relationship becomes sexual? Some women who have never had a conscious lesbian attraction in their life suddenly find themselves sexually involved with a woman they thought was just a "good friend."[16]

In a similar vein, Dr. Nicolosi states, "Some lesbians do not suffer so much from unfulfilled basic identification needs as from unfulfilled longings for nurturance. These women retain an unconscious need to repair a fragile mother-daughter bond."[17] A lesbian may feel that the only time she feels she is loved and cared for is when she is involved sexually with another woman.

Dr. Nicolosi provides some significant insight into women who

> seem to develop normally as girls, and in fact, function well heterosexually and marry, but then, to the complete surprise of their entire family, fall into a lesbian relationship in adulthood . . . the emotionally fragile woman with unfulfilled nurturance needs may turn to a

lesbian relationship out of disappointment and loneliness or after she has become disillusioned by a bad marriage or a divorce.[18]

Thus, lesbianism can be less predictable and may alternate during the woman's lifetime with heterosexuality.

In summary, we must come back to a position that bears repeating: Human development is quite complex. This complexity makes it nearly impossible to explain all the workings of the homosexual orientation for the male or female homosexual. There will always be exceptions to the factors. But my hope and prayer, and one of the reasons for writing this book, is that a greater recognition and understanding of some of the common factors that may have influenced our loved one's development of a homosexual orientation will encourage us to show a larger measure of compassion and motivate us to continue to reach out to him or her in love and prayer.

Chapter 9

Looking Back

Because of the complexities surrounding the issue of homosexuality and the many contributing factors that play a role in a person developing same-sex attractions, I think it would be unwise and even presumptuous for me to attempt to draw definite conclusions as to what may have specifically "caused" my son to develop a homosexual orientation. But when I look back over his childhood and adolescent years, I now can see many of the aforementioned common contributing factors were present in his growing-up years. In my reading and researching, I repeatedly saw an emphasis on the strong role the home and family life play in the development of a child. Though perhaps unintentional or even unavoidable, this may negatively affect the development of a child's personality and sexuality.

One of the questions parents often ask after learning their son or daughter has identified himself or herself as gay is, "How could one of my sons or daughters become a homosexual and none of his or her siblings develop that orientation when they all grew up in the same family with the same parents?" But if we look closely and honestly at our family life, we will see that the situations were not exactly the same for each child. Birth order can play a role, not only in how each child perceives his place in the family, but also, depending on age, how he or she is impacted by the various events that have occurred in the home. As stated earlier, a child's inborn temperament can play an important role in how he or she perceives and/or responds to situations in the home. The more sensitive the child, the more easily and deeply any real or perceived rejection by parents—or lack of favor in the parents' eyes—can wound.

Dan was the youngest of the three children in our family. Our first son, Nathan—or Nat as he was nicknamed very early—was born seven years before Danny, and in between the boys, we had a baby daughter who was stillborn at a pre-term delivery. Even in their infancy and toddler years, our two sons began to display their distinctive personalities. Nat was outgoing and confident, very much a "people person," easily making friends and quick to adjust to new situations. Danny was a very sensitive child, more reserved and shy, less confident, and slower to make new friends. Although both boys grew up in the same home and family, circumstances and events of their childhood years were significantly dissimilar and impacted the boys differently.

Their father, Jerry, had grown up in a broken, very dysfunctional home. When he was five years old, a bitter divorce between his mother and father, who was considerably older than she, resulted in Jerry becoming the pawn in the ongoing conflicts between them. During court-ordered summer custody visits, his father barely tolerated Jerry, demonstrated no love or affection toward him, and left him to fend for himself in a small apartment while he spent long hours away at his job. During Jerry's adolescent years, his mother remarried but made it very clear to her new husband that her son would always be first in her affections. Thus, there was no desire or effort by the stepfather to develop any kind of a father/son relationship with Jerry, once more denying him any opportunity to bond with a father or father figure. To make matters worse, the new husband was an alcoholic, and fights and chaotic conditions often erupted in the home.

I share this history regarding Dan's father because the lack of competent fathering in Jerry's life left him feeling ill-equipped and very inadequate to be a good father. During our engagement period, he confided to me, "I don't know what a good father is or what I need to do to be a good father, but I sure know what a bad father is and what not to do."

When Jerry first learned I was pregnant with Nat, he panicked, feeling overwhelmed with the potential responsibilities of fatherhood. He didn't even want me to tell anyone I was pregnant until my changing figure made the announcement unavoidable! But Jerry, though young in years, was a strong Christian and wanted to be a good father in spite of his fears. Thankfully, he quickly bonded to his newborn son, becoming a typical proud father and accepting his responsibilities to care for the new little addition to our family. As Nat grew older, Jerry enjoyed spending time with him, taking him places with him whenever possible, teaching him to play checkers and Monopoly, or roughhousing with him on the living room floor. During Nat's early childhood, we were very active with the Salvation Army as employees and as members, and our participation in the Army's many activities regularly exposed Nat to scores of different people, especially the young men in the youth group. These opportunities for Nat to interact in his early years with a large variety of people on a regular basis impacted his developing personality in a strong and positive way.

After losing our baby daughter through stillbirth, Jerry and I were both excited when we learned I was finally pregnant again, and we looked forward to the birth of another child. This time, Jerry was eager to tell people I was expecting, and Nat was excited about being a big brother. However, when Danny was born, our home situation was less settled than it had been at Nat's birth. The Salvation Army officers with whom we had served for so many years had been transferred to another city, both Jerry and I had recently changed jobs, and at the same time, we began to attend a different church.

I had stayed home from work for eighteen months after Nat's birth, but financial pressures necessitated my going back to work only three months after Danny was born. It was difficult to find someone to care for a three-month-old baby, and finally, I reluctantly left him with a young mother whose husband was attending a local college. I say reluctantly because I didn't know this family and the situation in the home appeared somewhat disordered. I wasn't sure if the young mother, with two small children of her own, would be able to give enough special time to Danny, but there seemed to be no other options.

I still vividly remember my emotional struggle over having to go back to work and not being home with my infant son. One morning as I was bathing Danny, I began to weep, the tears streaming down my face and dripping into his bathwater. The thought of having to put my son into someone else's care—even if it was only during my work hours each day—was tearing me apart. I'm sure Danny was not neglected by his new caretaker, but *I* wanted to take care of him instead of leaving him in the care of a stranger. After a number of months, I was able to make more satisfactory arrangements with a loving, Christian family who immediately "adopted" Danny and gave him their affectionate attention. But I have sometimes wondered if those few but critical early months interrupted the nurturing so vital to Danny's development and sense of well-being.

Bob Davies and Lori Rentzel write of the importance of these early years in an infant's life in their book *Coming Out of Homosexuality*:

> As soon as we can see, hear and feel—at birth or even in the womb—we begin taking in information that tells us who we are. Long before we can articulate our feelings or even have an organized thought, we can sense peace, warmth, comfort, love. We can also detect disturbance, tension, anger and fear . . . While the events of these early years do not *cause* us to become lesbian or homosexual, they can set the stage for problems to develop later in life. Ideally, an infant's first year or two of life is spent developing a deep, secure bond of love with the mother that leads to a *healthy sense of personal identity*. Psychologist Erik Erickson calls this the development of "basic trust." . . . With a solid sense of identity and a confidence that his or her need for love

and care will be met, a child has a good foundation for future growth and development. When this foundation is disrupted, the child is vulnerable to all kinds of problems.[1]

Nat eagerly anticipated the coming of a new baby into our family and made no secret of the fact that he wanted a baby brother. When Danny was born, Nat was ecstatic and proudly proclaimed to everyone that he now had that little brother. But it soon became evident that the seven-year age difference made it difficult for the two boys to play together or enjoy common activities, and Danny was often the annoying little brother bothering his big brother's stuff.

Things seemed to come easy for Nat. He did well in school, and his amiable personality, accompanied by his quick wit, made him popular with his peers as well as adults. That can create a challenging situation for a younger brother who is less extroverted and who may grow up feeling he is walking in his older brother's shadow. During the writing of this book, Dan confirmed to me how he viewed his older brother: "Nat was always the Golden Boy."

The biggest difference in our home in the early lives of our sons was the absence of Jerry from the home when Danny was very young. During Nat's infancy and early childhood, Jerry was available to spend both quantity and quality time with him, and consequently, a strong bond developed between them. The situation was quite different with Danny. When Danny was two years old, Jerry accepted a position with a Christian company that presented patriotic and drug education assembly programs in middle and high schools throughout the state of Florida. Jerry's responsibility was to contact principals to book programs, which required him to travel a good portion of each week. Nat was nine years old by then and could understand why his father was going away and when he would return. In fact, he found his father's work exciting and was thrilled to meet the guys in the band that presented the programs. Danny, however, was too young to comprehend why his father kept leaving or to know that he would surely return. How did his young mind perceive the repeated departures of his father? Did he see it as his father abandoning or rejecting him for some reason?

Jerry's traveling job and away-from-home schedule continued for about two years. Shortly after that, a family crisis arose which again required Jerry to be away from his family. Jerry was an only child, and when Danny was four years old, Jerry's mother was stricken with lung cancer. She was living in Ohio and was divorced from her second husband. Her only source of income was a small garage-door business that she managed out of her home. Since Jerry was between jobs, we agreed he should go to Ohio to maintain the business while his mother was undergoing chemo and radiation treatments.

At the time, I was employed by a large airline that provided pass privileges for my family and me, allowing Jerry to make frequent trips back from Ohio to Miami where we lived. He would be gone to Ohio for a maximum of three weeks, fly home for an extended weekend, and then return to Ohio for another two or three weeks. At the time, it was a necessary sacrifice for our family in order to keep his mother afloat financially during her recovery from cancer. This long-distance responsibility for my husband continued for about six to eight months.

We had no way of knowing that Jerry's absence as a father over this three- to four-year period had the potential of negatively affecting Danny's relationship with his father. By the time Danny was born, Jerry had already bonded strongly with Danny's older brother. There was never any intention or even awareness on Jerry's part to be less bonded with Danny. But his absences from home came at a very critical time in his young son's life. It was only many years later, when I was searching for answers to how my son had developed same-sex attractions, that I learned the crucial importance of a young child bonding to his/her same-sex parent in the critical early years of childhood. A disruption in that essential bonding process can contribute to gender-identity conflict.

During Jerry's absence, Danny naturally bonded even more strongly with me. After Jerry was back in the home and active in

Danny's life again, everything returned to normal, or so we thought. Although I began to notice that Danny did not seem to have the same close relationship with his father as his older brother did, I didn't attach the significance to it that I should have. I thought as Danny grew older and began to be more actively involved with his father, their relationship would deepen. Jerry did play board games with Danny just as he had with Nat, and I have memories of Danny and his dad lying on the living room floor as Jerry taught him to play checkers. However, many years later, when I shared those memories with Dan, I was taken aback by his response, "Daddy never played checkers with me."

I tried to prod his memory, thinking surely he remembered those times because they were not infrequent occasions. But Dan continued to insist that he and his dad had never played checkers. Those memories were gone from his mind. While that may not seem all that significant in and of itself, I couldn't help but wonder if the lack of recall of those memories was a product of the alienation he had felt from his father. In one of our discussions after Dan told me he was gay, he remarked, "I never felt close to Daddy. I always thought he was closer to Nat than me."

Dan's statement did not come as a shock to me, having observed the close relationship of Nat to his father, but it did grieve me to know that Dan had grown up with a feeling of being less loved by his father than he perceived his older brother was. What did shock me, however, was when Dan confessed to me that he always thought *I* loved Nat more than him! I was crushed to learn that had been his conclusion. The thought had never entered my mind! What had I done or not done that could have communicated that misconception to Dan? I knew how important it was not to favor one child over another, and to the best of my understanding, I had not done so, but somehow that was the message that came across to Dan—that I loved his brother more.

In an earlier chapter, I referenced the important role of perception; the way a person perceives a situation or a relationship, even if the perception is incorrect, becomes his reality—what he believes to be true. He then emotionally responds out of that reality. I was completely unaware of Danny's incorrect perception of my love for him. When I later shared Dan's statement with my good friend Jan, she was also taken aback that Danny thought this. Her reaction was, "If you preferred one son over the other, I would have said it was Danny, not Nat. You seemed to give him more time, more attention." But that was not how Dan perceived it.

My voice filled with emotion as I immediately sought to correct Dan's faulty assumption. "Oh, son, that's not true. I never loved Nat more than you. I loved you both very much. And I am so sorry if somehow I did not communicate that clearly to you and for the pain and insecurity that must have caused you."

Dan's courageous revelation of his long-hidden feelings was like opening a window to his soul, allowing me to look inside and see the ache and longing buried there. The knowledge that he carried the hurt and destructive weight of feeling less loved by not only his father but by me broke my heart. The more I learned of the sense of isolation and emotional pain in my son's life, the more my compassion for him grew and the more I understood the wisdom of an important truth. Coming to know the emotional pain in the homosexual's life does not make the homosexual behavior less wrong; it just makes it more understandable.

Is there any value in taking a look back at the past? For me, I believe there was. I desperately wanted answers for myself and for Danny. The "born gay" premise had been satisfactorily refuted for me in the early days of my search for answers, and I also had come to understand that Danny did not choose to be gay. The attraction he felt to his own sex was not something he wanted or had consciously chosen.

One day, as Dan and I were talking on the phone, I was able to tell him that I now understood he had not chosen to have homosexual attractions. For a moment, there was silence on his end of the phone, and then he replied softly, "I can't believe you are saying that." His voice conveyed the deep relief my words gave him.

I began to understand some of the struggle and anguish these attractions had brought my son. The accumulation of information that I had gathered from knowledgeable sources dealing with the issue of homosexuality had been extremely helpful, but I thought I needed to apply this information personally to our family, to try to identify events and relationships that might have negatively and harmfully impacted Danny, wounding him in ways I was not aware of and had not previously understood. I also needed to try to settle my personal struggle with guilt, feeling that somehow, unknowingly and unintentionally, I might have failed my son and contributed to his becoming a homosexual.

Were there things that I had done or not done as a parent that had played a part in Dan developing same-sex attractions and adopting a homosexual identity? Had his father and I somehow failed to "do it right" as parents? I knew our desire had been first of all to have a strong, Christian marriage, centered on the Lord Jesus Christ, and then, on that solid foundation, to establish a loving, Christian home and family and raise our sons to know and love the Lord.

That was our desire, but in reality were we able to do that? Did we consistently display the character of Christ in our words and actions? Did we always make wise and loving decisions as parents? In all honesty, I knew the answer to these questions was a big unequivocal NO. In spite of our good intentions and honest desires, we were not perfect parents. We didn't have all the answers or knowledge we needed, nor did we always understand clearly how to properly apply what we did know. At times, we reacted to situations out of our emotions and not out of godly wisdom and patience. Although we were both Christians and wanted to do what was right, we were both still flawed, imperfect, and yes, sinful people with incomplete knowledge, doing some things right, doing some things wrong, and sometimes leaving undone things we should have done. We were like all parents—imperfect. My own relief came when I was able to accept the truth that there are no perfect parents on this earth, and that includes Christian parents.

I have often said, "I wish I had known when we were raising our children what I know now. There were things I would have done differently." I would have been more intentional in teaching my sons God's Word and spiritual truths and less inclined to assume they would gain them naturally through the process of osmosis from Jerry and me. God instructed his people in the Old Testament to diligently teach his truths to their children, to talk about them when they sat at home, when they walked along the road, when they lay down, and when they got up (Deuteronomy 6:7). I wish I had more intentionally and consistently done that. I would have more frequently told my sons how much I loved them, how very precious they were to me, so hopefully they would have never doubted it and would have always felt secure in my love.

There are things about child development I wish I had known. I wish I had been aware of the factors that can contribute to homosexuality in a child's life, but the word *homosexuality* was hardly in my vocabulary at that time. I wish I had recognized the red flags that I now can identify in Dan's early life and realized the potential damage they could cause. And most of all, I wish I had been aware of the sexual abuse when it first started and had been able to protect my son from its damaging effects.

While acknowledging the obvious—there are no perfect families and no perfect parents—we must at the same time emphasize the importance of the family's influence on each of its members and encourage others to make every effort to structure family life on the principles of God's Word. Michael R. Saia gives this strong reminder of the importance of the family: "Our family background affects what we think about ourselves, other people, and even God himself. And since our behavior proceeds from our thoughts, our entire lives can be influenced by family relations."[2]

When I look back, I can identify with Joe Dallas's description of the father in the biblical account of the prodigal son:

> If there were warning signs, the father didn't see them. And
> if he had seen them, he probably wouldn't have guessed

what they meant. So by the time he knew there was a problem . . . he was clueless as to what had gone wrong.[3]

"Looking back" can be helpful if we gain insight and clarity in dealing with our own situation. It can also be futile, because the past is the past; it cannot be changed or wished away. And we have to be careful not to assign blame where no blame is warranted. There are often unavoidable circumstances and traumas in life that can cause disruption in the family and lay the groundwork for wounds, insecurities, or unfilled emotional needs in some family members.

It is important not to let ourselves become trapped in a self-defeating and potentially destructive guilt trip. Feelings of guilt and blame are a typical and understandable first reaction for parents; probably every parent struggles with these feelings when first learning their child is identifying him- or herself as gay. After all, aren't parents primarily responsible for the well-being of their child, assuring he or she will grow up to be a responsible and morally upright adult? If something goes wrong, it must be the parents' fault. As I've already shared, this was certainly my initial reaction and struggle. But this conclusion is an unwise and unnecessary assumption of full blame on the part of parents. We must objectively and realistically address feelings of guilt so they do not conquer and cripple us.

We have to quit beating ourselves up. We need to acknowledge our failures or inadequacies, ask our child's forgiveness if necessary or appropriate, but then turn loose of the past. The past is past; we can learn from it, but then we must move on or else our continuing to carry the weight of guilt will consume and paralyze us. The New Testament gives us wise counsel in this regard. "But one thing I do: forgetting what lies behind and straining forward to what lies ahead" (Philippians 3:13b ESV).

There is a vivid metaphor in the New Testament (1 Peter 5:8) that describes Satan not only as the enemy of God's people but also as a roaring lion who prowls around looking for someone to devour. We need to recognize that Satan would very much like to eat us alive with guilt. We must therefore learn to stand against him with truth and God's enabling. Ultimately, our older teenagers and adult children are responsible for their own actions and choices. We recognize that same-sex attractions are not a choice for them, but their homosexual activity is.

Joe Dallas, in addressing the role of the family and whether imperfections of the parents "caused" a son or daughter to become homosexual, reminds us that homosexuality is not caused by one influence alone. He concludes that based on all available research, there are at least five factors that can influence the development of same-sex attractions:

1. The child's genes (whether or not he's been born with a genetic susceptibility to gender-identity problems) combined with:
2. His relationship with his parents combined with:
3. His relationship with siblings and peers combined with:
4. Possible violations or traumas combined with:
5. Other factors we are still unaware of.

Perhaps some or all of the above, but not one of these alone, create the homosexual orientation.

Dallas goes on to say, "A parent's love cannot prevent destructive influences from affecting a daughter or son."[4] The following excerpt from his book gives instructive and comforting counsel to parents:

> What to do? If you can see where you're guilty of mistakes or wrongdoing as a parent, admit it, and take responsibility for it. You may have apologies or explanations to make to your son or daughter, and now would be a good

time to make them. But it's wrong to assume whatever mistakes you made *created* your son's or daughter's sexual preference. You may—or may not have—contributed to it. Your influence is limited; so limited that you could not, even if you wanted to, have caused your loved one's homosexuality . . . Be realistic when you assign blame. Take responsibility for whatever wrong you have done to your child, but refuse to accept responsibility for his sexual orientation and for what he has decided to do with it.[5]

In the early days of my struggle as a parent trying to come to grips with how much was I to blame for my son's homosexuality, I read somewhere that there has only ever been one perfect parent—God—and his kids (Adam and Eve) didn't turn out perfect! In spite of their Father's perfect love and wise, protective counsel ("Don't eat the fruit of the Tree of Knowledge of Good and Evil"), Adam and Eve, abusing their God-given gift of free will, chose to give in to their own desires and go down a path that would reap unimaginable, destructive, and painful consequences. It has brought me comfort to know that my Lord God, the perfect Father, knows and shares the pain of a parent who has to watch his child making decisions that are diametrically opposed to all the parent had planned, hoped, and prayed for, decisions that will ultimately bring them pain and disappointment. Because he knows and understands, Hebrews 4:16 can be a source of great encouragement. "Let us then approach the throne of grace with confidence, so that we may receive mercy and find grace to help us in our time of need."

Chapter 10

Coming Out of My Closet

There are times when familiar Scripture verses come alive with deeper meaning and significance as you see the reality of their truth undeniably demonstrated—sometimes in the ordinary events of the day, but often in times of crisis and deep need. The encouraging words of Proverbs 3:5-6 were already underlined in my Bible, but the words sprang to life for me when I so desperately needed help and guidance. "Trust in the LORD with all your heart and lean not on your own understanding; in all your ways acknowledge him and he will make your paths straight. [Or will direct your paths.]" Similarly, Proverbs 16:9 reminded me, "In his heart, a man plans his course [or way], but the LORD determines his steps."

When I first started down this new and unfamiliar path, I had no understanding of my own to "lean on." Realizing how much I needed information and direction, I cried out to the Lord for help and then had taken what seemed to be the obvious first step—obtaining books on the subject of homosexuality from a Christian perspective. As I planned my course of action, the Lord determined my steps and made sure I picked up not only the right books containing needed information, but a specific one that provided an unexpected additional resource. In the back of one of the books I bought that day at the Christian bookstore was a listing of Exodus ministries and their locations. My heart beat faster when I saw that one of the ministries, Worthy Creations, was located in Fort Lauderdale, the very city where my son and I lived at that time.

I wasted no time before contacting Worthy Creations and setting up an appointment with Richard Culbertson, the director of the ministry at that time. We made plans to meet a few nights later in the parking lot of a church where Worthy Creations' men's support group would meet that evening.

As Richard and I talked, he shared his personal testimony of struggling with same-sex attractions and the fifteen years he had spent in homosexual relationships. I was surprised to learn that for many of those years, Richard was a Christian; he had truly trusted Christ as his Savior earlier in his life but had continued to struggle with same-sex attractions and finally yielded to those desires. But now, because of his stronger desire and subsequent choice to live in obedience to the Lord and by the enabling grace of God to do so, he had walked in freedom from homosexual relationships for a number of years. He had grown in his love for the Lord and in his own healing to the point that he was able to help others who struggled with homosexuality but wanted to know the possibility of change and experience freedom from the bondage of homosexual practices.

We sat in his car and talked for over an hour until it was time for Richard to go to his meeting. I came away from our time together with helpful information, encouragement, and hope and was excited to learn that Worthy Creations sponsored a support group for families and friends of loved ones involved in homosexuality. Richard encouraged me to maintain a loving relationship with my son and not give up on him, and his testimony gave me hope. Actually meeting someone who had been actively involved in homosexual relationships but was now walking in freedom from that sexual addiction and living strongly for the Lord gave me hope that the Lord could do that in my son's life.

Remember the friend I mentioned earlier who had discovered her son was gay five years before I learned about Dan? She was one of the few people I had told about Dan, and when I learned there was a parents' support group in our area and invited her to go with me to a meeting, she jumped at the opportunity. We timidly made our way into the church where the group met and eventually located their room. The group was small in number, but the camaraderie, shared pain, and quest for answers and hope were quickly apparent and brought relief and comfort to my friend and me. The small group that night was mostly composed of parents, but there was a young girl present whose brother had recently come out to his family. At last! Here was a place we could freely tell our stories, here were others who understood our pain and disappointment, here were people who would pray with us for our loved ones and who would share our concern. Here also was a place we could learn about homosexuality. I felt I had been thrown a lifeline and eagerly looked forward to the meetings each week.

I attended the parents' group for several years, during which time only a few close friends knew of my involvement since I kept it a closely guarded secret. One day, I received a call from a friend whom I had known for many years but with whom I had only infrequent contact. She was teaching a weekly ladies' Bible study group in Fort Lauderdale and wanted me to come and share my testimony as part of their study on the sovereignty of God. My public testimony at that time was how God's faithfulness, love, and grace had sustained me during and after my husband's illness and subsequent death and then when the tragic and fatal motorcycle accident took my older son's life soon after. The strong truth of God's sovereignty was the spiritual rock that had kept me secure and given me hope during that time. My younger son's involvement in homosexuality was certainly not included in my testimony because, at that point, I was still struggling to climb back up on the rock of God's sovereignty.

I agreed to come and give my testimony, only to learn that her group met at the same church and on the same night as my parent support group. The obvious challenge was how to get to her meeting without her knowing I was already at the church for my own meeting whose purpose I definitely was not ready to reveal to others.

The night I was to give my testimony, I shared my dilemma with the rest of the parents' group, requesting their prayers. Then I drove my car to a different parking lot in the church closer to the building where the ladies' Bible study was meeting so if anyone saw me approaching, it would appear I had just arrived. I came and went with no one the wiser as to my dual purpose of being at the church that night. But each week after that, I was much more cautious of my comings and goings to the support meetings, always seeking to avoid coming in contact with my friend or any of the ladies in her Bible study group. More and more, I began to feel I was living a double life, believing I had to hide my life as a parent of a gay child. Can anyone else relate to that?

After a couple of years' participation in the parent group, I was asked by the original leader and founder of the support group if I would consider taking the leadership position. Both she and her husband were experiencing health problems, and she needed to step aside from her leadership role. At first, I didn't see any way I could take on that additional responsibility. I was heavily involved in my church, working long hours as the business administrator, teaching a singles class, and also serving as a coordinator for the Singles Ministry. But when I sought counsel from one of the ministers on the church staff (one of only two ministers who knew my closely guarded secret), he wisely advised me, "Ann, other people can take over the coordination of the Singles Ministry, but very few people are qualified to lead that parent support group. God has prepared you for the responsibility of that specific ministry."

I had to agree. As I looked back, I could see how the Lord, step by step, had been faithfully fulfilling what he had promised that dark Easter Sunday night several years earlier—that someday, after I had found healing for myself and had become more knowledgeable about homosexuality, I would be able to help others who were traveling behind me on this journey.

I had been involved in the parent group for some time but did not tell Dan of my involvement. Even after I was asked to take over leadership of the group, I refrained from sharing that piece of information with him. From comments he had made, I knew he had a negative opinion of Exodus and the people involved with their ministries. Based on his belief that homosexuals were born gay and could not change, his judgment of those who claimed to have come out of homosexuality was either they would eventually go back to homosexual relationships or that they were never really gay; rather, they were really heterosexuals and had just been "trying out" homosexual relationships. I guess I hesitated to tell him about my role in the family and friends support group because I was not sure how he would react to my involvement with an Exodus ministry. Since the parent group was more of a behind-the-scenes activity, I had decided it wasn't necessary to tell him.

But then I was asked to serve on the board of directors of Worthy Creations, which presented the possibility that I would be in a more public and visible role than just leading the parents' group, and I was concerned that might potentially create a problem for Dan. I wasn't sure it was fair to him for me to commit to that wider involvement without his awareness. This situation came up during the short period of time that Dan was seeing the Christian counselor, so I decided I would call the counselor and ask his advice on what I should do. Without any hesitation, the counselor advised, "Just ask Dan what he thinks about it. Tell him you have been asked to serve on this board, but you want to make sure it is all right with him, and that you won't do it if he doesn't want you to. Give him the opportunity to tell you how he feels about it."

I thought to myself, *What a novel idea!* In spite of having what I thought was a good, honest relationship with my son, I had not thought of being so open and direct with him on this subject. I began to pray that God would create a divinely appointed opportunity for me to ask Dan.

At Dan's suggestion, we had started having dinner together once a week. His reasoning was that he would like to have more time for us to be together and talk about what was going on in each of our lives. Of course, I was thrilled that he wanted to spend more time with me, and I looked forward each week to our dinner together in my home. I made sure to leave work in time to prepare our meal, or sometimes Dan came to the house early and had the meal ready when I walked in the door. On those nights, when I arrived at the house, I was greeted by the wonderfully tantalizing aroma of the meal he had prepared. He was becoming a very good cook, and it was a treat for this mother to eat her son's cooking. By the same token, he enjoyed eating a meal home-cooked by his mother on a regular basis. For Dan, those nights fulfilled his original desire for us to have time to talk together. For me, those nights were an unexpected blessing. It was a joy spending time with my son.

At one of our weekly meals, Dan made a request of me. "Mom, you've got to get Shirley off my back." (Shirley was a close, longtime friend of the family.) "She keeps asking me when I'm going to get married and have a family so we can have children at the house at Christmas time. Will you please tell her I'm gay and have no plans to get married and have children—ever?"

I knew what my answer had to be. "No, Dan. I won't tell her. If you want her to know, you need to tell her yourself. I'm not going to do that for you."

"Okay, I will. I really don't care who knows that I'm gay."

When I heard that statement from Dan, I immediately recognized that this was the God-created moment I had been waiting for to ask for Dan's permission for me to serve on the board of Worthy Creations.

Cautiously, I began. "Dan, there's something I need to talk to you about. I've been asked to serve on the advisory board of Worthy Creations, an Exodus ministry here in Fort Lauderdale. I want to know how you would feel about my being on the board. I will not accept the position if you don't want me to."

To my surprise and relief, Dan quickly responded, "Go ahead, Mom. That's okay with me. I don't mind if you do that."

Thinking this might be a good time to also tell him about my involvement with Worthy Creations' parent's group, I proceeded.

"There's something else I need to tell you. For some time now, I have been leading a parents' support group sponsored by Worthy Creations. It's a group that seeks to help parents, families, and friends know how to respond in a biblical way to a loved one who is gay."

Again, to my surprise, Dan didn't hesitate to give me a very supportive response. "I think that's great, Mom. You can help other parents understand that it's okay to still love their kids even though they're gay."

That night, the door of my self-imposed closet began inching open, and in the days and months ahead, God pushed the door wide open as he began calling and drawing me out to the assignments he had prepared for me. That night also set in place a pattern I would follow in the days and years to come. Before accepting opportunities or requests to speak or share publicly our story, I asked Dan's permission. I understood it was not just my testimony or story, but it was Dan's life too. It was *our* story.

The opportunity to test this new way of more openness with my son came very quickly. My recently acquired friend, Christine Sneeringer, was being asked more frequently to speak on the subject of homosexuality and had begun a four-week series of talks at a very large church near the church where I attended and served on staff. I was surprised when Christine phoned and asked me to give a presentation from a parent's perspective as a part of her four-week series.

Checking with Dan for his permission proved to be the easy part of the assignment. What I quickly remembered was that very few people in my church knew that my son was gay or that I led a parents' support group. How could I possibly speak at a church geographically near my church where the likelihood was great that someone from my church would learn about my being there and the subject of my presentation? It didn't seem right or fair that people from another church would learn my dark secret before my own church family did. Yet it seemed easier to talk to a room full of strangers who might never see me again than to tell my secret about my son to people I worked with every day or faced every week.

I had convinced myself the reason I was not telling people about Dan, especially at my church, was because I was protecting him. He still came to church with me occasionally, and I didn't want people looking at him in a curious, unaccepting—or worse, condemning—way. Sadly, I had heard a few unkind remarks about gays from some church members, and I didn't want anyone communicating disdain or rejection to my son.

But the Holy Spirit was not content to let me get by with that reasoning, which was somewhat selfish and not totally honest. It was true that a large part of the reason for my silence was that I wanted to protect my son. But with penetrating accuracy, God's Spirit revealed another deeper reason for my hesitancy to let people know about Dan. God began to peel back the outer protective layers of my heart to reveal the ugly pride rooted deep within me. I was not entirely motivated by a desire to protect Dan; I had to admit I was also concerned about what people would think about me if they knew I had a gay son. It was my Christian reputation I was trying to protect. I was afraid people would judge and condemn me as a failure; I was especially concerned that this would be the reaction from other Christian parents whose kids had "turned out" just fine.

When God showed me the reality of what was in my heart, it was painful and not a pretty picture. It sounded much more noble and self-sacrificial to say I was protecting my son from what others might think of him than to admit I actually was more concerned about what people would think of me. I needed to bow before the Lord, confess my own sinful attitude and reasoning, and ask for grace and courage to do what I knew he was setting before me. Before speaking at the neighboring church, I needed to tell the staff and a few others at my own church.

After praying for wisdom and courage, I decided I should start by sharing individually with the three ministers on staff who did not yet know about Dan's involvement in homosexuality. Then, in our weekly planning meeting, I shared the information with the six church secretaries whom I supervised. Breaking the silence was emotionally hard but, in a strange way, liberating at the same time.

There was another group I felt the Lord wanted me to meet with—a particular Promise Keepers group, one of several formed in our church after many of the men attended a large Promise Keepers convention. Most of the men in this particular small group served on church committees with whom I had worked in my capacity as church business administrator. One night as they gathered at the church for their weekly meeting, I asked if I could meet with them. They readily agreed, though puzzled as to my reasons. Through tears, I shared with them about Dan and how, out of fear and pride, I had hidden what I considered my own dark secret from my church family for several years. I explained how I felt God now wanted me to be open about it.

After I finished, I went back to my office to wrap up my work responsibilities and call it a day. I was emotionally drained. But before I could leave, one of the men from the meeting appeared at my door and said, "Ann, we just wanted you to know how much it meant to us that you were willing to share something so private and painful, and after you left, we prayed for your son. We wanted to commit to you that we will continue to pray for him and for you, and we believe that God is going to do great things in both your lives in the days ahead."

After he left, it dawned on me that each group or person I had shared with over the past few days had promised to pray for Dan and for me. By my willingness to be obedient to the Lord and to lay down my own pride and self-preservation, God was expanding the circle of those who would be praying for us. One more time, God was teaching me the importance of listening to his Spirit and obeying, even when I thought he was asking too much of me.

Gradually, the circle of those in my church who knew about Dan widened. When I was asked to be the speaker at our church's annual ladies retreat, the topic I chose was how God uses suffering to conform us to the image of his Son. Once more, I felt that gentle nudging from the Lord to be transparent and share with the ladies the grace and faithfulness of God to me after I learned of my son's homosexuality. There was no denying the painful struggle of the past few years, but there was also no denying how God was using the journey in a redemptive way toward his purpose of changing me to be more like him.

The retreat was held at a small resort center on Florida's west coast. God blessed us with beautiful, sunshiny weather and a soft breeze blowing in off the ocean. Wanting to take full advantage of the scenic setting, we held our first early-morning session outside on the patio, arranging our chairs in an intimate circle.

There were only about twenty-five ladies attending the retreat, most of whom I knew personally. I waited until I had almost finished teaching before I forewarned them that I was going to share something very personal. Tears spilled over and ran down my cheeks as I disclosed to them my son's embraced gay identity and homosexual involvement and my deep concerns for him. But thankfully, in spite of the emotions, God kept my voice under control. What I wanted the women to hear most was not my pain but God's faithfulness to me and what he was teaching me as I traveled this unforeseen new journey with my son.

My honest and unexpected revelations to them prompted a time of candid sharing from some of the other ladies about their own painful struggles during recent times of suffering. A sweet sense of God's presence permeated the circle as women opened their hearts to one another and shared God's faithfulness in the midst of life's pain. I sat back, amazed and humbled at how the Lord was drawing the ladies together in a close fellowship of shared suffering and encouraging all of us with the truth that he can use times of suffering for our good and his glory. The experience of that morning was another memorable "standing stone" in my life's journey.

But God wasn't finished yet; he had a few more plans to draw me completely out of the closet. Our pastor was planning a series of sermons on the cultural and social issues of our day, and to supplement his sermons, he wanted individuals who had experience with each issue to give a brief testimony. One of his subjects was homosexuality, and he asked me to give a short testimony in each of the two Sunday morning worship services about being the parent of a gay child. Talk about raising the bar!

Following my usual pattern, I talked to Dan about it and asked his permission to present this testimony before the whole church. This was a much larger and more personal venue than when I spoke at the other church, and once more, I wasn't sure what his feelings about it would be. Again, to my surprise and relief, he quickly assented, explaining, "Mom, I am confident there are people sitting in the pews in your church who are struggling with same-sex attractions or who are already involved in homosexual relationships or have family members who are. You can help these people, Mom. You need to do this."

He was right. On the Sunday I spoke, after both worship services, several people came up to me to share that they had family members who had come out as being gay, and they had not been sure how they should respond to them. Several said that what God had been teaching me gave them encouragement and challenged them to reach out in love and not just condemnation.

My son's continued positive responses and permission for me to speak publicly about his gay identity and what the Christian response to homosexuality should be was an unexpected but very welcome development. In many areas, we were coming from opposing viewpoints. He knew I would speak from a biblical view and he would not agree with everything I said. But he also knew I would emphasize the biblical message of Christ's love that Christians needed to display and would not focus solely on the sin of the behavior. He knew I had come to recognize that homosexuals did not choose attractions to their own sex; however, he also knew I would say those attractions did not justify the choice to satisfy those desires with wrong behavior. My understanding of these facts had helped me to see that it is possible and appropriate for parents, families, and friends of the gay-identified to display compassion without compromising biblical truths and standards. Dan clearly understood this was what I would be sharing with those hearing me speak.

It would have been understandable if Dan had adamantly refused to allow his life to be put on display. I am extremely proud of my son, not just for his willingness for me to be involved so publicly in this controversial arena, as that automatically involved him as well, but also for his concern for others and his encouragement for me to reach out to help other families who are dealing with this difficult issue. The foundation for his willingness may have been laid in those first few months of this unexpected journey when God strongly impressed upon my heart the importance of loving my son unconditionally and seeking to learn all I could about homosexuality. Remember, my prayer had been that God would help me see my son as he saw him, and later, God had extended that to Dan's partners and then on to others who identified themselves as gay.

I had prayed for wisdom and direction in keeping the bridge of communication open between Dan and me, and God was doing that. At first, both my son and I had benefited from my growing understanding of the pain and struggles in his life, and now others were benefiting as well.

But one troubling question—and perhaps the most difficult challenge of all—still had no answer and was yet to be faced: When and how do I tell my family? There was no one left to tell in my husband's family; both his parents were deceased, and the few remaining relatives had lost contact with me after Jerry's death. It was just my family, and although we were a close family, many miles separated Dan and me from them. With the exception of one brother and his family in Virginia, they all lived in Missouri, and Dan and I lived in south Florida. My mother was no longer able to travel, and visits from my brothers and their families were infrequent. Dan's full-time work schedule limited the visits he made with me to Missouri. With so many miles separating us, it was not difficult to continue hiding Dan's gay identity from the family. So I said nothing and postponed that inevitable and dreaded disclosure as long as I could.

But God in his providential working and timing introduced events into our lives that would not allow me to continue keeping the closet door closed to my family. At that time, Dan was working at Blockbuster's corporate headquarters in Fort Lauderdale. When the company decided to move its headquarters to Dallas, Texas, Dan—in order to keep his position—moved, along with his partner, to Dallas. (Interestingly, his move to Texas coincided with my increasing public involvement with homosexual-related ministry and opportunities to share our story in various venues.)

Shortly after Dan's move to Texas, my niece, who lived in Missouri and was a few years younger than Dan, contacted him to ask if she could come to Dallas for a weekend visit. Aware that Ann knew nothing of his gay identity or that he was living in a homosexual relationship, Dan panicked and immediately called me.

"Mom, Ann is insisting on making this trip to Dallas and, of course, is planning to stay at my apartment for the weekend. I've got to tell her I'm gay. I can't let her come not knowing and then be hit like an unexpected lightening bolt out of a nonthreatening sky with the reality of my gay partner and roommate! I'm going to tell her . . . and then she can come if she still wants to."

Immediately, I knew the time had come to tell my family. But I did not want my brother and his family to learn of Dan's gay identity from their daughter. I needed to be the one who broke this unexpected and probably shocking news to them.

I cautioned Dan, "Son, hold off on telling Ann. This is going to hit her like a bombshell, and I think it would be much better if I told Uncle John and Aunt Elaine about your situation and let them tell Ann. Then they can talk about it and decide whether Ann still wants to carry out her plans to visit you."

Dan readily agreed to this plan, and I suspect he was relieved when I volunteered to break the news to the family. For me, however, the prospect of delivering this difficult and what I thought would be totally unexpected information to my brother and sister-in-law, followed by telling two other brothers and their wives, was a daunting and dreaded chore. For five years, I had delayed and avoided telling my family. I had managed to keep what I considered my dark secret about Dan hidden from my family.

My reluctance to tell my brothers and their families that Dan—my son, their nephew and cousin—was identifying himself as gay and was in a homosexual relationship had been rooted in the uncertainty of how they would respond. I feared they might reject him and not want to continue a relationship with him. I worried that if they rejected Dan over the homosexual issue, he would cut off all contact with the family, and that would cause an even deeper wound than he already had experienced from broken and lost family relationships. He had no roots of family on his father's side, and I worried this revelation might destroy for him the family roots on my side of the family. My mother-heart wanted to protect my son from more emotional pain.

There was also the possibility that this could put a breach in my close bond with my brothers and their families. To my knowledge, no one else in our family had ever claimed to be gay, and homosexuality was not a subject that I could remember coming up for discussion in family gatherings. So with dragging feet and trembling hands, praying for wisdom for the right words and the ability to keep my emotions under control, I dialed my brother John's phone number, halfway hoping he wouldn't be home. But after a few rings, John answered the phone, and in a voice quivering with emotion, I told him I needed to talk to both him and Elaine about a serious matter, and I asked him to have her join us on the phone.

I wanted so much for them to hear my heart and not just my words. I desperately wanted to communicate to them not just the reality of the situation, but also the pain that I had come to understand Dan had struggled with for years and the betrayal and abuse he had experienced at the hands of a "friend." I told them I was not asking them to accept or condone Dan's homosexual behavior but was hopeful they would still accept and love Dan. I explained my reasons and concerns for not telling them about Dan sooner, but that their daughter Ann's announced plans to visit him in Texas had forced the issue.

To my immense relief, John and Elaine both assured me that, as much as the news shocked and saddened them, it did not change their love for Dan or their acceptance of him. He would always be welcome in their home. In view of Ann's intentions to visit Dan in the very near future, I asked if they would share this information about Dan with Ann (as well as their teenage son) and alert her to his living arrangements and then suggested they and Ann could make a decision about her visiting Dan in Texas. They agreed but could not promise what Ann's reaction would be to this unexpected information about her cousin. However, they assured me that even if Ann's reaction were negative, it would not change their feelings toward or decisions about Dan. They also assured me they would be praying for Dan and for me. I hung up, breathing a deep sigh of relief and giving thanks to the Lord for this outcome. One brother down, two to go!

Next I called my brother Jim and repeated to him and his wife, Barb, pretty much what I had shared with John and Elaine. Though still emotional, I was able to communicate to them what was on my heart and why I had not told them sooner, and that Ann's planned trip to visit Dan had brought the matter to a head. To my surprise, my disclosure did not come to them totally unexpected. They told me they had had a few questions concerning Dan but had not said anything to me. Thankfully, they too responded in love and acceptance toward Dan, assuring me they still loved him and that this would not change their relationship with him. I also asked them to share the information with their grown son and daughter. After thanking them for their compassionate and understanding response, I hung up the phone, feeling much reassured and proceeded to call Eddie, brother number three. I was determined to plow ahead and complete the difficult task of telling the family about Dan.

My phone call to my brother Eddie and his wife, Pam, repeated the pattern of the first two calls, and I was met with the same understanding and compassionate response. Afterward, I heaved a big sigh of relief and had to acknowledge, to my own regret, that I had badly misjudged the way my brothers and their families might respond. In retrospect, I wished that I had not waited so long to tell them. My heart was overflowing with gratitude to the Lord for the blessing of strong support from my immediate family. I knew from my years of involvement with the parent group that not all families responded in such an accepting manner, and that families often became fractured or even torn apart by the coming out of a family member.

I decided, however, that there was no need to extend my announcement of Dan's homosexuality to other family members. That could wait until a later time. I also decided there was no good reason to say anything to my mother about Dan. By this time, Mother was in her late eighties and exhibiting early stages of dementia. I thought it best to spare her the difficulty she might have processing this disturbing information about her grandson and the resulting pain and worry it would bring her.

Addendum: Ann did make the trip to Texas to visit Dan, and any initial awkwardness quickly dissipated as they enjoyed together her first visit to the Dallas/Fort Worth area.

Chapter 11

Family Matters

"Mom, how do you think Daddy would have responded to my being gay?"

A number of months had passed since Dan had revealed to me that he was gay. He had stopped by the house to spend some time with me when, out of the blue, he pitched this question at me. It caught me by surprise but evidently was something Dan had been mulling over in his mind. Had his dad still been alive how would he have reacted to his younger son's announcement he was gay?

I could understand how Dan might have that question since he was just entering his adolescent years when his father died, and as I had learned, Dan's perception was that his father was closer to his older brother Nat than he was to him. How *would* his father have reacted when he learned that his younger son was identifying himself as gay and was involved in a homosexual relationship? Would he have been able to still love and accept him, or would he have reacted in anger and rejection?

Knowing it was important to answer Dan as honestly as I could, I tried to respond thoughtfully and with sensitivity. "Honey, I think at first your daddy would have struggled with this knowledge, just like I have. But I think in some ways it would have been even more difficult for him. For some reason, fathers seem to have a harder time dealing with the revelation of their son's homosexuality than mothers do. But because of your father's strong relationship with the Lord and his knowledge of God's Word, I think he would have been able, after some time, to come to the same position I have. There would be disappointment, pain, and grief, but I think he would have continued to love you and accept you as his son. At the same time, I believe he would have told you your homosexual behavior is wrong. Then, just like I have, I think he would have tried to learn all he could about same-sex attractions and would have tried to understand your struggle."

Though Dan did not ask any more questions at that time, I later wondered how his older brother, Nat, would have responded had he learned that his younger brother was gay. I was glad Dan hadn't posed that question because I did not have the answer.

When I began to attend the meetings of Worthy Creations' parent and family support group, I quickly became aware that my family situation was different than most others who have to deal with the unexpected revelation that their child or sibling is dealing with same-sex attractions and may already be involved in a homosexual relationship. By the time Dan came out to me, I had been widowed for thirteen years, and it had been ten years since Nat had been killed in the motorcycle accident. Dan was my only surviving child, so it was just the two of us who initially had to work through this painful and difficult time. As I've already shared, we were geographically separated by many miles from all other family, so I could postpone telling any of them about Dan.

In some respects, there was both an advantage and a disadvantage in our unusual situation. The advantage was that it minimized the complications of interacting with other family members on a regular basis and dealing with their possible negative reactions. The disadvantage was it increased my painful sense of aloneness and isolation as I struggled to move on down the road of life after this unexpected sharp turn in a new and distressing direction.

The Manner of Disclosure

How a family learns of the gay identity of a family member can differ immensely. There may be some early red flags that raise concerns or at least some speculative questions in the minds of family members, or the discovery may come crashing in like an earthquake, creating emotional havoc. For some parents, there may have been an isolated and momentary thought that unexpectedly pushed itself into their mind about the possibility of their child being gay, but it was quickly brushed away like an annoying, dangling strand of a spider web. For others, a gnawing worry may have chiseled away at the edge of their consciousness for years, long ignored, but finally and painfully confirmed.

Dan's shocking disclosure that Easter Sunday afternoon caught me totally off guard. I didn't have a clue that my son was gay. He certainly didn't look like I thought gays would look; he had no obvious feminine mannerisms and was not flamboyant in dress or actions. He was not out marching in gay parades and sure didn't have a big H on the front of his shirt. During his high school years, he had gone steady with a girl for three years and following graduation from high school had expressed interest in an attractive young lady he met at work. When his interest in her began to wane and I questioned him about it, his response was, "Mom, she lives all the way on the other side of Fort Lauderdale. That's too far to drive."

Since that was only about a twenty-minute drive from where we lived, I smiled and in a teasing way responded, "I'll swim the deepest ocean, climb the highest mountain, but don't ask me to drive to the other side of Fort Lauderdale." Dan grinned but said nothing.

Some time later, there had been that one brief moment when it dawned on me that Danny had not dated or expressed an interest in any girl for a considerable length of time. That annoying word *homosexual* flashed briefly in my mind, but not wanting to even entertain that possibility, I had brushed the word away so quickly it had no time to implant itself. It was only later, when I was struggling with the reality of Dan's embraced homosexuality, the faint memory of that brief moment resurfaced.

In some cases, as with my son, parents hear directly from their son or daughter the shocking announcement of their homosexuality.

Later, in my search for answers, I read that it is a more positive situation when the son or daughter breaks the news themselves to their parents or another family member than when they learn of it in another way. The direct disclosure may be an indication of trust or respect for the parent or family member and may signal the desire for a continued good relationship with the parents and hopefully other family members. I believe that was the case with my son when he was finally able to tell me, and I grasped at this thin thread of comfort. Sometimes the son or daughter will first disclose their secret to a sibling or another family member with whom they have a close relationship and will then enlist their help in telling others in the family.

Some parents may learn the devastating revelation from others outside the family or—perhaps even more difficult to cope with—may unexpectedly and quite accidently find homosexual materials in the possession of their son or daughter.

For Barbara Johnson (author of *Where Does a Mother Go to Resign?*), there was no forewarning or subtle clues from her youngest son Larry, who had recently graduated from high school with multiple honors and awards. While looking for a book that one of her son's friends called to borrow, Mrs. Johnson received the shock of her life when she discovered in her son's desk drawer a large stash of homosexual materials—pictures of nude men, magazines advertising homosexual films, and assorted information on homosexuality. The unbelievable and disgusting discovery hurled her into a cavernous pit of disbelief, panic, and gut-wrenching emotions and then into deep depression.

But whatever the vehicle on which the unwelcome news arrives, it usually leaves behind personal devastation for the parents and the gnawing fear that family life has just been changed forever, and not for the better.

Making the decision to disclose homosexual involvement to one's family and then carrying through with that decision may be the most difficult thing a son or daughter has ever done. But afterward, the child may feel a sense of relief because his or her inner struggle has been externalized. However, for the parent, the pain has just begun, and their own pain at hearing this news often prevents them from being sensitive to the pain their child experienced in telling them.

Identifying the Pieces of the Puzzle

One important piece of information that needs to be determined at the time of disclosure is: Where is your loved one on the broad spectrum of homosexuality? Is he or she just confiding to you that he or she thinks he or she *may* be gay and wants clarification and help? Is he or she struggling with same-sex attractions but has never acted upon them, or is he or she already involved in homosexual activity and the homosexual community and perhaps even has a partner? Knowing the depth of the loved one's involvement in homosexuality is a valuable piece of the puzzle and will give some insight as to how parents can respond and proceed.

If your loved one is not yet involved in homosexual activities or practices, he or she may be much more open to help, such as going to a counselor, talking with someone who has experience in ministering to those struggling with same-sex attractions, or even attending—perhaps with you or another family member—one of several ministry conferences offered each year on this subject. However, if they are already involved in homosexual activities and are not looking for help but are just coming out to you, the situation is more complex and your options more limited.

Another factor that will definitely influence the response and actions of a parent is whether your child is still a teenager or perhaps even younger. If he or she is still under your authority in the home, you have every right to set courses of action that will provide information and help, like getting counseling from a Christian therapist who has knowledge and understanding of same-sex orientation or contacting ministries such as Harvest USA (*www.harvestusa.org*), Restored

Hope Network (www.*restoredhopenetwork.com*), or Living Hope Ministries (*www.livinghope.org*) for information and direction. The parent also has the responsibility and authority to set boundaries for unacceptable behavior in the home in the same way you would for any other unacceptable behavior.

If your loved one is open to help, stand ready to support him or her and provide informed, biblically centered help. Wherever your loved one is on the homosexual spectrum, whatever his or her age, by God's enabling grace, assure him or her of your love and that you want to understand his or her struggle.

The Uniqueness of Each Family

While families may share some common denominators, each family situation is unique. What is the makeup of the family? What is the members' history together? Is the parent a single parent, divorced, or widowed? What is the relationship of the husband and wife? Do they have a close, loving relationship or is it strained and fractured? Are there other siblings, either still young enough to be in the home, or grown adults, who may be married and have families of their own? Does the extended family (grandparents, uncles and aunts, cousins, nieces and nephews) live close by with many opportunities for interaction or are they separated by geographical distance and rarely see each other? What family dynamics and relationships are already in play?

And a very important consideration and distinction is: What is the spiritual condition of the home and the individual members in the home or extended family? Once the initial shock of the disclosure has subsided somewhat, will their reactions and attitudes toward the gay family member be shaped and determined by a desire to respond in a biblical, God-pleasing way? Will they be able to continue demonstrating acceptance, love, and compassion *without* compromising the biblical view of homosexual behavior?

Or will their reaction be based on a preconceived, negative view and prejudgment of all homosexuals and include an insistence that they want absolutely nothing to do with the gay family member? A third possibility is that some in the family will have embraced the prevalent view of homosexuality reflected in our current culture—that a person is born gay, they are just being who they are, and other people have no right to judge them or say that their sexual behavior is wrong.

Often the initial and difficult questions for the parent(s) to face and decide are, *Who* do we tell, *when* do we tell them, and *how* will they react? Reactions from family members will probably vary, so it's often not possible to predict ahead of time what each family member's reaction will be. Reactions toward the gay family member can range all the way from loving acceptance to anger, disgust, and total rejection, and the parent(s) should try to prepare themselves emotionally and spiritually, as best they can, for these varying responses to their announcement to other family members.

To help with this preparation, I want to reiterate some foundational statements I made back in chapters four and five:

- It is important that very early on this new journey parents come to understand and embrace a biblical position on the issue of homosexuality, not only in their response toward their loved one personally but also toward their sexual behavior. A solid biblical understanding can then give us a secure foundation on which to make the many decisions we will face in our relationship not only with our son or daughter but also with their partners and will provide guidance on how we should respond to the whole homosexual issue and those who identify themselves as gay. A strong conviction of the correct biblical position on homosexuality and the ability to articulate that conviction in a firm but compassionate and loving way not only will better equip you to more clearly communicate the startling news to the family but also to properly respond to various reactions from family members.

- Your own close, personal relationship with the Lord is vital in dealing with exchanges between different family members and responding to their varied reactions. Make it your first priority to strengthen your own personal relationship with God through time in his Word and in prayer. You will need his guidance, wisdom, strength, direction from his Word, encouragement, perseverance, and hope for this journey. Bathe each situation in prayer before approaching individual family members. Depend on God to give you strength and godly wisdom and to prepare their hearts to receive and accept this news about their loved one that will likely be unexpected. Trust God to create the right time and opportunity to talk with them and to give you appropriate words and a proper response regardless of their reaction. Even after all your preparation, when all is said and done—depending on the reaction—you may need to run to the Lord to be your strong tower to be strengthened by his comfort and never-failing love.

The name of the LORD is a strong tower; the righteous run to it and are safe. (Proverbs 18:10)

God is our refuge and strength, a very present help in trouble. (Psalm 46:1 ESV)

The nature of the relationship to the gay-identified family member can also influence a person's reaction. Learning that someone you know or love is a homosexual can unleash intense emotions. The closeness of the relationship, the nature of the history of the relationship, and the frequency of contact with the gay-identified relative can all impact how a family member may react to the knowledge that a loved one is now identifying him- or herself as homosexual.

Sadly, the revelation of the homosexuality of a family member can often bring about strained or broken relationships within a family, and parents are often caught in the middle. They may be put in the position of having to choose with whom they will stand—their son or daughter or the opposing family member. An older sibling or a sibling's spouse may take the position that they want nothing to do with the gay family member and refuse to come to family gatherings if he (or she) is going to be there. They may refuse to allow their young children to be around the gay-identified family member. Parents can attempt to clearly and patiently share information about the development of same-sex attractions and the need for compassion toward a loved one who struggles with these issues. They can try to explain that it's possible to do this without accepting the wrong sexual behavior, and that totally rejecting the loved one only brings them more pain. Perhaps the withdrawing relative might be open to reading an informative and helpful book, such as the excellent one by Joe Dallas, *When Homosexuality Hits Home: What to Do When a Loved One Says They're Gay*. But because homosexuality is often a deeply emotional and sometimes explosive issue for people, the opposing family member may not be willing to listen or be open to helpful information.

When this happens, parents are faced with an extremely difficult and painful choice. Will they feel pressured or compelled to succumb to the threats of the opposing family member and agree to exclude their gay loved one from family gatherings, or will they make the equally painful decision to continue to stand in love with their gay child, risking the very real possibility of the withdrawal of the other family member— and possibly his or her entire family—from future family events?

I cannot speak from experience in this area since I was spared the pain of having to deal with any strong rejection from family members toward my son, but I heard many heart-wrenching stories from parents in Worthy Creations' parent and family group and can genuinely empathize with parents who do have to face the intense pain of ruptures in family relationships. The fear of my family rejecting Dan and the deep emotional pain that would cause him and me was a major reason I delayed telling my brothers and their families about Dan.

If the overtures for reconciliation continue to be rejected, the parents' response may have to be, "I'm sorry you feel that way, and it causes me great pain to see the family separated by this situation, but I will not disown, reject, or exclude him (or her) from family gatherings. I do not condone his (or her) sexual behavior; it is wrong and unnatural, but his (or her) wrong choices of behavior do not obliterate my love for him (or her). I would feel the same way toward you if you became involved in some kind of wrong or immoral behavior. The door will continue to be open for you to participate in the family gatherings if you should choose to do so."

And then you pray for God's continued wisdom and direction in this situation, for him to work in the hearts and minds of all involved, and wait and hope for an eventual reconciliation.

You also continue to show love and acceptance to the dissenting family member, perhaps making special plans to invite them for dinner or another special event at another time.

The most difficult situation to face may be if the parents are divided about how they are going to respond to their gay child. This can put tremendous strain on the relationship between a husband and wife. In this situation, it may be wise and helpful for both parents, if possible, to consult with a qualified Christian counselor who can be an objective third party and bring his or her knowledge, wisdom, and experience to the situation. Make sure that the counselor you choose is not only a Christian but also one who has some knowledge and understanding of homosexual issues.

Accept Me Totally or Else!

Another factor that can complicate family relationships is the attitude of your loved one when he or she makes this very personal and difficult disclosure to the family. His or her attitude may be defensive, belligerent, or demanding. He or she may have already accepted the position of the more vocal and uncompromising pro-homosexual advocates. He or she may demand not just acceptance as an individual but also acceptance of his or her same-sex behavior. He or she may see your rejection of behavior as rejection of them. He or she may throw down the gauntlet from the very beginning—total acceptance of his or her homosexuality and homosexual practices. He or she may demand that his or her homosexual partner be accepted into the family as you would that of an opposite sex partner of a heterosexual child, not only by you but by the whole family. He or she may insist his or her partner be included in all family functions, and that he or she and the partner be given the rights and privileges of a married couple, including sharing the same bedroom when they stay overnight. The culmination of these demands may be a threat to cut off all communication with the family if the demands are not met.

Understandably, the hope and deep desire of most parents is to preserve a good relationship with their child. This does not mean, however, that the parent has to succumb to demands that would violate his or her own convictions and standards. If these demands are being made of you, even though your child may now be an adult, you do still have the right to stand firm on your own Christian convictions and establish moral boundaries in your own home. Your loved one's inconsiderate and defiant attitude may well arouse your own anger and defensiveness, but it is important to state your position in a forthright and firm manner as calmly and lovingly as possible.

- Make very clear that you love your son or daughter and that you will continue to do so, but that—just as when they were a little child—loving him or her does not mean that you will allow or accept wrong behavior. State that you will not abdicate your right to maintain Christian standards of behavior in your home, noting that your responsibility is first to the Lord and obedience to his Word. Therefore, homosexual behavior or inappropriate homosexual materials will not be allowed in your home. Their sexual relationship is wrong, and you have the right to not allow that behavior in your home. Communicate that the partner is welcome in your home (assuming you've been able to reach this point!), but sleeping arrangements will always be in separate rooms. Explain that this would be your same position if his or her partner were of the opposite sex. You will accept his or her partner as someone you can befriend and love, but you will not accept or condone their homosexual relationship. Also, you cannot dictate or control how other family members will react to the relationship, but you will not allow any demands from your gay son or daughter to be placed on them.

- Stress that you will always love him or her and that you want very much to preserve family relationships, but some things are nonnegotiable. Tell him or her you understand that he or she has the right to make his or her own decisions, and you will respect that right, but you hope that he or she will also respect your right to stand true to your firmly held convictions. Emphasize that even though you may disagree on this issue, you very much want to maintain a loving relationship. Hopefully, this will also be the deep inner desire of your loved one, but sadly, sometimes the end result of these very difficult conversations may be an angry or bitter response from your loved one, and the interchange may conclude with his or her storming out of the house, vowing never to return. Like the father of the prodigal son, even though your heart is breaking, you have to let him or her go. But if this happens, remember, by God's enabling grace, you can relinquish him or her into the hands of your heavenly Father, who loves your prodigal far more than you are capable of loving him or her, and as you pray, he will relentlessly pursue him or her with his care and love.

Thankfully, my son spared me the horrendous pain of hearing and standing against unrealistic ultimatums. He wanted to preserve our close relationship as much as I did. Beginning with our first conversation that Easter Sunday afternoon, God enabled me to exhibit a loving stance toward him but at the same time take an uncompromising biblical stand against his homosexual behavior and relationships.

Several months later, Dan unexpectedly revealed to me how he actually felt about my "love without compromise" position. I was taken aback when he declared, "Mom, I'm glad you responded like you did when I told you I was gay. If you had responded any other way, I would have lost respect for you."

His statement spoke volumes to me, for it revealed that deep down in his own heart, even though he had firmly embraced a homosexual identity for himself and did not share my view that homosexual behavior was inherently wrong, he had not expected me to deviate from or abandon my own core beliefs and values. In fact, my doing so would have destroyed his respect for me—a vital element of our good relationship. It would also have communicated to him that my allegiance to Jesus Christ and his Word was not as authentic as I professed, weakening in his eyes the reality of the gospel and perhaps diminishing the desirability of a relationship with Jesus Christ for his own life.

I say this to encourage parents who may be wavering in this area. Compromising true biblical standards so as not to lose your son or daughter is never a winner. While it may temporarily keep him or her from walking out the door at that point in time or may appear to preserve the relationship, it can ultimately destroy the credibility of biblical truth in his or her eyes. You will face other crucial decisions further down the road, perhaps whether to attend his or her wedding or civil union ceremony. Taking and maintaining a strong but loving biblical position from the very beginning lays a foundation on which to make other decisions regarding your loved one as other situations arise.

Perhaps out of shock and an intense emotional reaction to the disclosure of your gay-identified child that loving element was missing from your initial reaction. You may have even hurled Bible verses at him or her, letting him or her know in no uncertain terms how much the Bible condemns homosexuality—that God called it an abomination! But hopefully, when cooler heads prevail, the opportunity will still be there to go back to your family member and add the missing ingredient of love, acknowledging to him or her that love is an essential element of a true biblical position. Don't let pride keep you from apologizing to your child and asking his or her forgiveness for your initial unloving response.

Once more, I would direct parents and family members to *When Homosexuality Hits Home: What to Do When a Loved One Says They're Gay*, an excellent book written by Joe Dallas and published by Harvest House Publishers in 2004. From his many years' experience addressing these issues, Dallas is able to write in greater detail in some areas than I have and covers areas and situations I have not included in this writing. Because of his counseling proficiency, he gives some very specific professional advice to follow in many situations.

Important Role of the Parent and Family Support Group

I cannot emphasize enough the importance of parents developing or maintaining a growing, intimate relationship with the Lord Jesus to equip them for this journey. When parents or family members first came to the Worthy Creations parents and family support group in Fort Lauderdale, they were deeply wounded, distraught, often angry, and desperately looking for answers to help them "fix" their homosexual loved one. This was certainly understandable. However, one of the first things we shared with them was that their first priority, strangely enough, was not for their gay child. They must first fix themselves!

Their first priority was their own relationship with Jesus Christ. It is essential for parents to have the solid assurance that they know Jesus Christ as their Savior. Then, out of a growing, strong, intimate relationship with Jesus Christ can come healing for their own pain, wisdom for the many decisions they will face, and daily strength for the journey that lies ahead. They need to know unequivocally that the Lord can be their refuge and strong tower when they are wounded or overwhelmed. "The LORD is a refuge for the oppressed, a stronghold in times of trouble. Those who know your name will trust in you, for you, LORD, have never forsaken those who seek you" (Psalm 9:9-10).

Parents will need to know what God's Word teaches so they can live by its truth and make wise, biblical decisions. They will need the encouragement, direction, and strength that God's Word gives. To help meet this need, each meeting of our parents' group included a short devotion or Bible study, and parents were encouraged to have their own daily time in God's Word. The faith of even the strongest Christian can be tested and become strained during the extremely difficult trials of life, so faith must grow and be regularly strengthened by God's Word and prayer.

Another important component of our meetings was the opportunity to share our stories. The meetings usually began with a brief time of sharing. For many of the parents, this was the only place they could openly and honestly tell their stories and know that everyone there understood and supported them. They could also get feedback and benefit from the experiences of others in the group who were walking ahead of them on this unfamiliar road.

Most of the parents were like I was—totally uninformed and ignorant about homosexuality. It was something they never dreamed they would have to deal with in their families. For the most part, they knew nothing about the factors that may have contributed to the same-sex attractions that developed in their loved one. Parents needed to be equipped with accurate information to understand the struggle their loved one has endured and wounds of life they have suffered so they could respond to them with empathy and compassion. Therefore, an important segment of the meetings was devoted to educating ourselves on these issues.

We also stressed that *we* did not have the ability to change our loved ones; rather, that is God's job. We emphasized that just as parents' first need is for a strong relationship with the Lord, that is also the first need of their gay loved one. Only the almighty, powerful God, through the ministry of the Holy Spirit working in hearts and lives, can bring about spiritual change or growth and—hopefully, eventually—a desire to change one's sexual behavior. The change must begin inwardly from which outward change can follow. Our part is to live an authentic Christian life, visible to our loved ones, and to work with the Holy Spirit by praying. In our parents' group, strong emphasis always was given to the importance and power of prayer, and at the end of each meeting, we held hands, formed a prayer circle, and prayed together for our loved ones.

I discovered in my years of leading a parent/family support group that more often than not it was the mother of the gay child who actively looked for help and made the initial contact with Worthy Creations. Fathers were more likely to stay in denial or simply did not want to get involved with a support group. As a result, it was a rarity when the first call for help came from the father.

One Man's Story

A memorable exception was the father who made the first contact with Worthy Creations himself. As was the custom, the office of Worthy Creations always referred any calls from parents to me, so Jack was given my office phone number at the church where I worked, and he made the call. Jack's son had just come out to his father and stepmother, and Jack's reaction was first one of disbelief and then pure rage. It was unbelievable and totally unacceptable to him that *his* son could be gay. Jack was a "man's man" of strong Irish descent who had been a boxer in his younger days. He had a strong disdain, even repulsion, for gay men. The thought that his son could be attracted to his own sex was a totally foreign, disgusting concept that triggered strong anger as well as deep embarrassment at the thought of his own equally manly brothers learning this about his son.

Jack confessed that he wanted to find his son's partner and beat him up. Having been a boxer earlier in life and in the heat of his anger that seemed like a logical plan. But Jack was a Christian, and to his credit, he was desperately looking for answers and was open to help. When I encouraged Jack and his wife to come to the next meeting of the parents and family support group, he immediately agreed to do so. However, I thought it best to forewarn him, "You may be the only man there," and sure enough he was. But in spite of being the only man at many of the meetings and having to drive a long distance to attend, Jack and his wife Charlene kept coming to the meetings. And at his first meeting, one of the things he heard was "The first thing God wants to change is you."

Over time, God did a miraculous transforming work in Jack's heart. He began melting the hardness of his heart toward his son and replaced his anger with love. Jack had experienced God's love in his own life, and the Holy Spirit was able to open his eyes to see that God had that same love for his gay-identified son and for all others who identify themselves as homosexuals. Just as God had worked in my own experience, God began to burden Jack's heart that he not only was to show God's love to his son but to his partner as well. What was truly amazing was that when the first Christmas rolled around, Jack and Charlene were able, by God's grace, to invite their son's partner to their home for Christmas dinner. What is even more amazing is that God gave Jack a strong desire to reach out to those who were struggling with same-sex attractions and were open for help to change.

Jack and Charlene were driving about an hour each way to come to the biweekly meetings. At that time, we were the only functioning parent and family support group in south Florida, and gradually several other parents from Jack and Charlene's area also began to make the long drive to Fort Lauderdale in order to come to a parent support group. As I watched the transforming work God was doing in Jack, I began to suspect that God might be preparing Jack for something in the future. After one of the parents' meetings, I spoke to Jack privately and shared my thoughts with him. "There seems to be a growing need for a parents' group in the West Palm Beach area, and I think God may be preparing you to lead it."

God's plans for Jack and Charlene were bigger than mine. At the writing of this book, Jack and Charlene have both retired from their jobs and are leading the growing "Family Ties" ministry in Boyton Beach, Florida, which not only ministers to families who have a loved one who has come out as gay but also offers counseling and support to both men and women who are struggling with same-sex attractions and looking for hope and help.

Parent and family support groups are an invaluable resource when someone you love is gay-identified. If there is a ministry in your area that reaches out to those struggling with same-sex attractions or wanting to escape the bondage of their homosexual practices, check to see if it includes a family support group. If it does not and one is not located within a reasonable driving distance, the ministry can still provide valuable information and phone support to families and friends.

Another resource is the Waiting Room ministry, which exists and specializes to help hurting families impacted by homosexuality. It includes Waiting Room Online, a valuable resource for families who do not have a family support group in their area. Information can be found on their website, *www.WaitingRoomMinistry.org*.

It is important to intentionally seek out help and support, to know that you are not alone and that help is available. Who knows what God may have planned for you after you find your own healing and help? God is an awesome God! You may be the instrument he wants to use to help other hurting families or to reach out to those struggling with homosexuality. I would never have dreamed on that dark, Easter Sunday night that this was his plan for me!

Chapter 12

Partners: A Package Deal?

By the time a son or daughter discloses their gay identity to his or her parents or another member of the family, he or she may already be involved in a homosexual relationship. The parents are then immediately faced with determining not only their reaction to their son or daughter's homosexual identity but also how they are going to react to the partner.

As I shared earlier, after I came to understand the importance of loving my son unconditionally with God's kind of love, God began to impress upon me that I also needed to reach out in love to his partner Matt. He and any partners who might follow him needed to see God's love for them, demonstrated through my attitudes and actions toward them. Admittedly, this was not an assignment I was eager to embrace, but God does not ask us to do anything he does not equip us to do. "Now may the God of peace . . . equip you with everything good that you may do his will" (Hebrews 13:20 ESV). If I was willing to be obedient, God would fulfill his promise to empower me to do what he was asking me to do.

For many parents, even being willing to love their child's partner is difficult, and at first, may seem impossible. The very thought of their son or daughter being sexually involved with a person of the same sex can immediately put a barrier in their hearts and minds toward the partner. Also, as it was in my experience, the tendency can be to blame the partner for the relationship—"It's his/her fault, not my child's!"—and therefore resent him or her. Sometimes the reaction is not just blame but also anger or disgust toward the partner, with a strong aversion to even meeting him or her. The thought of allowing him or her in their home is totally out of the question. Left on their own, parents would need a miracle to have a kind and loving relationship with their loved one's partner. But as I was to discover personally, with God *all* things are possible.

When Dan unexpectedly broke the news to me about his homosexuality, my initial reaction, understandably, was purely emotional. The news unleashed a tangled mixture of shock, disbelief, denial, disappointment, and pain in my heart and apprehension for what lay ahead.

My own deep needs drove me to God and his Word, not just for solace but also for answers. Many of the passages I had read often in the past, but now God was opening my eyes to a better understanding of his unconditional love for *all* people, a love so deep and purposeful that he was willing to give his Son to die to pay for the sin of all mankind, collectively and for every individual in particular, so that he could make us his own and adopt us into his family. I came to understand that God's love and acceptance for my son was not determined or diminished by Dan's immoral sexual practices but was based solely on his great worth and value to God. He was created in the image of God, and even though that image—like that of all mankind—had been marred by sin, he was still precious to God and desired by him. Those truths helped me understand that I did not have to condone or accept my son's sinful sexual behavior, but that I could and should accept *him* fully as my precious child and, with God's enabling, love him unconditionally.

I have purposely placed this chapter on partners at a later point in the book because when we are faced with the prospect and challenge of accepting and loving our child's same-sex partner, we need to keep in mind that all the knowledge and insight we may have gained about God's love, homosexuality, and the needs of our own child must now be similarly applied to how we view our loved one's partner. What is of utmost importance to remember about the partner is that he or she is someone God values and deeply loves, and he desires to demonstrate that love through us.

Admittedly, the first meeting with a partner can be awkward and uncomfortable. The well-timed advice that Barbara Johnson gave me over the phone when I was filled with anxiety about Dan's first partner, Matt, coming over for dinner proved to be especially helpful and bears repeating: "Try not to think of him as just your son's sexual partner but as someone your son cares about. There must be some good qualities about him that attracted your son to him. Try to focus on those. Even more importantly, see him as someone God loves and to whom he wants to show that love through you."

When we think about how we can relate to our loved one's same-sex partner, it is important to recognize that not all homosexuals fit into the same mold. There is no such thing as a "typical" homosexual. One of the things that troubled me when I learned my son was identifying as a homosexual was the images that came to mind when I heard that word. I had seen pictures in the news of gay pride parades with half-dressed participants, usually male. I had read of the increasing ultimatums of gays demanding not just tolerance for their immoral lifestyle but also acceptance of their sexual behavior as normal and legitimate and equating demands for their gay rights to the civil rights movement. I knew that anyone who disagreed with their demands or dared to say that homosexual behavior was morally wrong was labeled "homophobic" or a "hate-monger."

My son did not seem to fit that image, but was this what he would eventually be like? Or was this perhaps how his partner was? And what about the gay agenda that seems to be growing in presence and scope—the concerted and aggressive push by some in the homosexual community to influence what is being taught in public schools, how homosexual relationships are treated by our laws, and to use other avenues to promote their belief that homosexuality is just another acceptable lifestyle? Were my son and his partner part of those activities?

Providentially, very early in my journey, Worthy Creations brought Joe Dallas to Fort Lauderdale to conduct a one-day seminar on the subject of homosexuality. One of his sessions was a real eye-opener for me as he shared that it is important to recognize not all homosexuals are in the same place in their thinking and lifestyle.

To illustrate this, Joe very broadly identified three different groups of homosexuals. I'm going to use some of Joe's description of these three groups and recommend for your further reading the chapter, "Understanding the Three Degrees of Homosexuality," written by Randy Thomas from Joe Dallas's material and included in the book *God's Grace and the Homosexual Next Door.*

The Repentant Homosexual

There are a wide variety of people in this group. These are homosexuals who do not want their same-sex attractions. They may have been raised in the church or come from Christian homes; they know that homosexuality is looked upon by most people as unnatural and sinful, but for as long as they can remember, they have been aware of and struggled with same-sex attractions. They may even have prayed that God would take these attractions and desires away. But on the other hand, they have heard from the gay community that they were born this way, and they should just accept it because they can't change. They may even have given in to the attractions and become involved in homosexual activity, but deep inside they are hoping and wishing for a way out. They do not want to live this way the rest of their lives. They are searching, open to help and hope . . . and to the gospel message of God's love and redemption.

The Moderate Homosexual

This is the category that most gays would probably identify with. They live responsible lives, hold down jobs, often are financially secure, may be in a long-term relationship, and may even consider themselves "married" to that partner, even if the relationship has no legal status conferred by the state. They are good neighbors and usually very pleasant, likeable persons. Most believe they were born gay and have accepted as fact that they cannot change, so they are trying to make the best of it. They want to be treated on an equal basis in employment opportunities and be judged by their abilities and work history, not their sexuality. Many moderate homosexuals do not want to be a part of the gay activism that is so vocal, and they may actually be embarrassed by militant gays who claim to speak on behalf of all homosexuals, by exhibitionists who march in gay pride parades, and by protestors who spew forth messages of intolerance, even hate, toward those who disagree with them.

The Militant Homosexual

Even though this is a small subset of those who call themselves homosexuals, it is a powerful and often affluent group. To quote Randy Thomas, this group has "moved beyond the days of simply wanting people to tolerate what they may not personally accept. They want to force acceptance of homosexuality and punish anyone who will not adopt their pro-homosexual ideology."[1]

As I listened to Joe Dallas that day at the seminar, it was not difficult for me to recognize that my son could be classified as a moderate homosexual. The partners he has had would also fit into that same classification. My conclusion was substantiated when Dan and Matt began to attend the Metropolitan Community Church in Fort Lauderdale (the official "gay" church), and a few months later, I asked Dan if they were still attending. His answer was enlightening. "No, we quit going. The church services put too much emphasis on activism for gay causes, and that's not what I went to church to hear."

Your gay loved one and his or her partner can probably be broadly identified in one of the above three categories—where and how they fit into those categories will influence how you relate to and interact with them. As Christians, we are called to love all homosexuals, but we may relate to them on different levels, depending on where they are and how they identify themselves. We are not called to accept the aggressive programs being pushed by the more militant factions of the homosexual community.

In the seminar, Dallas pointed out that we can and should stand against what is morally wrong in the homosexual arena. But we need to always stand in *grace and love* toward the *persons*. We should seek to understand what has brought the angry, defiant homosexual to this point. I was especially impressed by one statement made by Dallas that the homosexual who is the angriest may very well be the person who has been hurt the most in life and has experienced the deepest pain. The ongoing challenge for the Christian is to take a strong stand on issues that are adverse to the teachings of the Bible but to do that in *truth and grace.*

Over the many years of Dan's involvement in homosexual relationships, he has had only four partners. Early in each relationship, Dan told his partner, "My mom will be nice and kind to you. She will accept you and love you, probably invite you to dinner, but she does not accept or approve of our relationship. She believes it is morally wrong." I'm not sure specifically what else he told them, but they seemed to know I was a Christian and that I believed the Bible still has relevance and authority for our lives today. In some ways, this set the stage for me to extend a hand of friendship to his partners. However, it also raised the bar for me, challenging me to live an authentic Christian life before them and to demonstrate the truths and relevance of God's Word in my interactions with them. Dan's third partner in particular was very open to that. (More about that later.)

Initially, Dan truly believed that he and his first partner Matt would be together forever. He shared with me that, based on the long-term, stable, committed relationship of his father and me, he thought that was the way all committed relationships were supposed to be. Matt was a rather quiet young man, and although I never got to know him well, he seemed like a decent and likeable person. He and Dan seemed to be getting along okay, but after only a couple of years, he and Matt broke up. Evidently, as time passed, Dan became disillusioned with the relationship because he later told me, "My relationship with Matt was a joke." Clearly, it was not what he initially envisioned it would be.

Dan's next partner was Andrew, a handsome young man with an outgoing and congenial personality, as I discovered when Dan brought him to the house for dinner. Dan seemed to genuinely care for Andrew but soon discovered he had a few character flaws. First, money began to disappear from Dan's wallet. Then a few of his personal items were missing. Finally, when his camera was missing, he confronted Andrew about the missing money and articles, especially the camera. Andrew admitted he had taken the money and articles and had pawned the camera because he needed money. Dan did not want to break up with Andrew, so he forgave him. But he did disclose to me what Andrew had done.

Shortly after that, Andrew asked Dan if he could borrow his car to go to South Carolina since Andrew's car was not in good enough condition to make that long a trip. Dan knew I was planning a road trip about that same time and would be spending the weekend in Atlanta before traveling on to West Virginia. So he and Andrew decided that Andrew could drive back from South Carolina by way of Atlanta. The plan was for Dan to ride with me to Atlanta where I would drop him off at the home of a friend. Andrew would meet him there, and they would ride back to Fort Lauderdale together.

Dan called to tell me about the plan and asked if I thought it was okay to let Andrew take his car to South Carolina. Even after learning of his thievery, I had continued to treat Andrew kindly but no longer trusted him. I was honest with Dan and expressed my reservations about loaning Andrew his car, but acknowledged that Dan was an adult, it was his car, and he would have to make the decision. I was not going to tell him what to do.

However, the mother-bear instinct and concern for her cub rose up in me, and I decided it was an appropriate time to show some tough love to Andrew. I asked Dan to put Andrew on the phone, which he did. Kindly but clearly and firmly, I told him, "Andrew, Dan is an adult, and it's his car. It's his decision whether to let you borrow it. However, you know that in the past, you've betrayed Dan's trust on several occasions, and that has damaged my ability to trust you now. Trust is a fragile thing, Andrew, and once broken, it cannot be easily restored. I'm not going to tell Dan he cannot let you borrow his car, but I will tell you this. If you do not have Dan's car back to him in Atlanta by the time you say you will be there, I personally will call the police and report the car stolen. Is that clear? Do we have an understanding?"

Andrew meekly replied, "Yes, ma'am," and the car was back in Atlanta—on time. My firm and confrontational manner was not my usual approach with people, but love sometimes must take a tough stand, even with partners. I recently heard Beth Moore, a well-known Bible teacher and leader in women's ministry, make this statement when speaking at a conference, "Kindness does not mean weakness."

Your interaction with your loved one's partner may differ from partner to partner, depending on the position of the partner in the wide spectrum of homosexuality, how much he or she is willing to respond to your overtures of love and acceptance, and how much involvement your own loved one is willing for you to have with his or her partner. But whatever the situation, it is possible for you to make every effort to stand in an attitude of love and kindness. The apostle Paul gave this advice to the Christians in Rome, which I believe applies to "partner" situations: "If possible, so far as it depends on you, live peaceably with all" (Romans 12:18 ESV).

When Dan and Andrew eventually broke up, Dan was emotionally devastated, similar to husbands and wives who experience divorce. When I saw the very real pain the separation was causing him, I had to recognize the deep emotional bond Dan had with Andrew, in spite of his taking advantage of Dan during the time they were together.

The split also revealed to me Dan's fear of being left alone in life, which was understandable since he had already lost both his father and his brother by the time he was sixteen. The fear of abandonment is common in the human experience and is intensified when we have previously faced losses of people we love. During this very emotionally difficult time, Dan agreed to see a Christian therapist that I recommended.

When we first learn our loved one is involved in a same-sex relationship, we tend to think that the relationship is only about sex. And that might appear to be the case in some situations, especially for male homosexuals where promiscuity is more common. But there is also a strong emotional component in these relationships. Deep within every human being is an intense, legitimate, emotional need to belong to someone, to love and be loved, to have a close, intimate bond with another human being.

Ideally, these emotional needs are met in normal, legitimate relationships, first through parents and families, close friendships, and eventually, for most people, in marriage. However, as discussed in earlier chapters, when these legitimate emotional needs are not met and when other factors that can contribute to development of same-sex deficit are present, the emotional needs can become sexualized and acted out through sexual activity with the same sex. God designed the physical act of sex as the ultimate intimacy, but only between a husband and wife. The longing for deep sexual intimacy is a legitimate emotional need, but if the vehicle for meeting that need is illegitimate, ultimately the satisfaction is short-lived and brings further emotional emptiness and wounding. It is important to keep in mind that the illegitimate vehicle is not limited to same-sex sexual activity but also includes sexual activity with the opposite sex outside God's established boundary of marriage.

Also important to remember is that while fulfillment of sexual intimacy is a legitimate human longing, it is not an absolute necessity in order for a person to live a full and satisfied life, contrary to what our sex-saturated culture would have us believe. Whether a person is single by divorce, death of a spouse, or never married, it is possible to live a life of celibacy. Celibacy does not mean there are no sexual desires or longings for sexual intimacy. It simply means the person recognizes that he or she has the power of choice and chooses (maybe only by God's grace and empowerment) not to fulfill those longings illegitimately. Many can testify to this, including myself. My husband died when I was only forty-three, and at the writing of this book, I have been widowed for thirty-four years and have lived a celibate life. To apply this to the person who is attracted to his own sex—while not denying or minimizing the intensity of his desires—it is possible to choose *not* to surrender to strong sexual desires but instead to deliberately choose to live a celibate life. Many victorious "strugglers" can testify to this reality.

The normal longing for deep intimacy and the undeniable, pleasurable experience of a sexual union are both powerful forces, and when these two legitimate longings are expressed outside the boundaries God has established, self-deception is often the unrecognized fruit of the union. Dr. Robert Gagnon makes the statement, "Few areas are so given to self-deception as the area of sexuality. Where the potential for pleasure is greatest, the potential for clever and self-serving sophistry [subtly deceptive reasoning] is also greatest."[2]

Remember that Satan, the enemy of God, is also called the Deceiver (Rev. 12:9), and just as he deceived Eve in the garden, he still seeks to entice people to make wrong and destructive decisions by placing before them forbidden fruit and making it appear acceptable and alluring. It's much like a line from a popular song a few years back that went like this: "How can something that feels so right be so wrong?"

In trying to understand same-sex partner relationships, we need to recognize the powerful forces at work—the quest to meet legitimate emotional needs colliding with powerful sexual desires, both of which are a part of our human complexity. Added to this mix, Satan, the enemy of man's soul, strives to deceive us into believing that a loving union that seems to satisfy both legitimate emotional and sexual needs cannot be wrong. This is the position taken by many gays and lesbians today—a belief shared by a growing number of heterosexuals. They argue that the Bible does not condemn loving, committed relationships but only violent sexual activity, such as same-sex rape or excessively promiscuous same-sex behavior. As shown in chapter four, the Bible does not make those distinctions. It is the act itself that is condemned as sinful, whatever the setting. Quoting Dr. Gagnon again, "Forms of sexual expression that deviate from the kind of heterosexual union validated by God at creation can never, by definition, legitimately be construed as 'loving.'"[3]

Short-Term Nature of Same-Sex Partnerships

Statistics bear out the short-term nature of most same-sex partnerships for both male and female homosexuals. Peter Sprigg, senior fellow for policy studies of the Family Research Council, has compiled some compelling statistics on homosexual relationships in the brochure "Top Ten Myths of Homosexuality," available on the Family Research Council website *www.frc.org*:

> Homosexuals are less likely to enter into a committed relationship, less likely to be sexually faithful to a partner, even if they have one and are less likely to remain committed for a lifetime, than are heterosexuals. They also experience higher rates of domestic violence than heterosexual married couples.[4]

Sprigg supports this fact with results from several extensive studies. One study showed homosexuals (especially men) are less likely to be faithful to their partner.

> A Canadian study of homosexual men who had been in committed relationships lasting longer than one year found

that only 25 percent of those interviewed reported being monogamous. According to a study author Barry Adam, "Gay culture allows men to explore different . . . forms of relationships besides the monogamy coveted by heterosexuals."[5]

Sprigg concludes, "Homosexual relationships tend to be of shorter duration and much less likely to last a lifetime than heterosexual ones (especially heterosexual marriages)."[6] A 2005 journal article cites one large-scale longitudinal study comparing the dissolution rates of heterosexual married couples, heterosexual cohabiting couples, homosexual couples, and lesbian couples:

> On the basis of the responses to the follow-up survey, the percentage of dissolved couples was 4% (heterosexual married couples), 13% (homosexual couples), and 18% (lesbian couples). In other words, the dissolution rate of homosexual couples during the period of this study was *more than three times* that of heterosexual married couples and the dissolution rate of lesbian couples was *more than four-fold* that of heterosexual married couples.[7]

In the early days of my search for information about homosexuality, some of the information I read was more frightening than comforting. I read about the high rates of alcoholism, drug use, and promiscuity in the homosexual population and the unhealthy sexual practices that increased the risk of sexually transmitted diseases and other serious health issues. These factors could contribute to a shorter lifespan for those actively involved in homosexual practices, particularly those male homosexuals who tend to be more promiscuous, have multiple partners, engage in frequent one-night stands, and rarely live for a prolonged period faithful to one partner.

Over the intervening years, I have personally talked with several men who formerly engaged in same-sex activity. They told me they lost count of the number of men they had sex with over a period of years, including some whose names they never even knew. More often than not, these types of individuals are also involved in the use and abuse of addictive substances, such as drugs or alcohol.

This information triggered fearful concerns for me. Was this the lifestyle my son was involved in? Or had his partner been involved in any of these practices that would potentially harm my son?

Later, I learned that while all the above is sadly found in the homosexual culture, it is not true of all homosexuals. As stated earlier, the spectrum of those identifying themselves as gay is very broad, and their lifestyles can vary greatly. It is important for parents not to assume the worst but to try to find out from their loved one just where he or she and the partner are on the spectrum and not be consumed by unwarranted fears. In a nonconfrontational, nonaccusatory way, express your fears and concerns to your loved one and ask if they are warranted or not.

Early on, I confessed to my son that I was afraid the next thing I would learn about him was that he was HIV-positive or already had AIDS. Dan's reaction was prompt and forceful. "Mom, you don't have to worry about that. I'm careful, and I get tested every six months." He paused for a moment and then quickly demanded, "What do you think I am? Out having one-night stands? Mom, I'm not like that!"

"I'm truly relieved to hear that, son, but I'm not sure *what* I know about you anymore. I thought I knew you, but I'm learning there is much I didn't know. I love you very much, and the possibility of losing you to AIDS or some other destructive illness because of your homosexual behavior weighs heavily on me." Dan continued trying to ease my concerns by assuring me he was not involved in risky behaviors. Having a better understanding of his situation did help alleviate some of my fears.

Dan's third partner, John Michael, was a very personable, charming, and creative young man. The first time Dan invited me over for dinner shortly after he and John Michael moved into their rented house, I quickly realized John Michael was an excellent cook, and any meal prepared by him would be something to be savored. Since he was a devoted follower of Martha Stewart, he not only could prepare a delicious dinner but also served the food appealingly arranged on the dinner plate, set on a table that had been attractively decorated.

Conversation flowed effortlessly with John Michael, and on my second or third dinner visit in their home, John Michael surprised me when he started asking questions about the Bible and what I believed about God. This set the pattern for future dinner visits, and frequently John Michael would say to Dan, "Invite your mom over for dinner. I'll cook!" While John Michael finalized his meal preparations in the kitchen, I sat at the counter dividing the kitchen and dining area and answered the spiritually oriented questions John Michael directed to me. Dan would sit quietly by, listening to our conversation. When I realized this was going to be a pattern for my visits, I began taking my Bible with me, opening it on the counter to read appropriate verses to John Michael in answer to his questions. John Michael never ran out of questions, and I was thrilled with this turn of events and the opportunity to talk with him about the Lord.

But after a year or so, Dan's relationship with John Michael turned rocky, and disagreements and quarrelling became more frequent. When Dan told me John Michael would be moving out, I asked him if he minded if I contacted John Michael to continue the friendship that had begun to develop between us. To be honest, I wasn't sure how Dan would feel about that since he and John Michael were not parting on the best of terms and knew that if he was uncomfortable with my being friends with John Michael, I should not pursue it. But by this time, it was evident God was at work in John Michael's mind and heart, and I very much wanted to have further conversations with him. I prayed that if this was God's plan and timing, he would move Dan's heart to agree to my request. Thankfully, Dan responded, "I don't care. I'll give you his phone number if you want it."

I wasn't sure how John Michael would react to my overture for continued contact with him, but much to my delight, when I phoned him, he was obviously pleased and readily agreed to see me again. We made plans to meet at a T.G.I. Friday's for dinner (appropriately on a Friday night), and that was the beginning of a regular routine of meeting every few months at the same restaurant on a Friday night. For some unexplainable reason, we were always directed to the same booth, no matter which greeter seated us. We jokingly began to call it "our booth." It soon became apparent that our purpose for meeting at the restaurant was more than just to eat a meal and stay in touch. Our dinners were times of serious conversations, mostly about God and the teachings of the Bible. The sincere questions John Michael continued to ask confirmed that his thirst for honest answers about life and God and his search to determine the trustworthiness of God's Word were genuine. When I shared the nature of John Michael's and my conversations with Dan, he initially discounted John Michael's sincerity and claimed John Michael was just telling me what I wanted to hear. But deep in my heart, I knew this was not the case.

I wouldn't have been surprised if Friday's had put a plaque with John Michael's and my names on it over the booth we regularly occupied at the restaurant because we spent several hours there each time. Those meetings continued for a couple of years, and in the process, the friendship between us deepened.

Interestingly, in all those hours of talking, the subject of homosexuality never came up. I felt strongly that was not the main issue. Rather, my purpose in spending time with John Michael was to come to know him as a friend and share the truths of God's Word, the love of God for him personally, and the reality of a personal relationship with Jesus Christ. If John Michael had brought up the subject of homosexuality, I would have openly discussed it with him, trusting God for the right words; but he did not, and I did not feel God was leading me that way either.

Instead, little by little, I shared with John Michael the good news that it is possible to have a personal relationship with Jesus Christ, and that everyone, including me, is a sinner in need of a Savior and God's forgiveness. Out of God's great love for us, he sent Jesus into the world to die on the cross for us to pay the price for our sins, and the resurrection of Jesus from the dead is proof that the payment for sin had been made in full. I shared my own testimony with John Michael, not only of my salvation as a young child but also of God's faithfulness throughout my life, especially during some painful times of loss. I wanted John Michael to understand that Christianity is not just a set of beliefs but also a very personal and intimate relationship with God our Father through his Son Jesus Christ.

Shortly after John Michael and I began our Friday meetings, Blockbuster Corporation, where my son was employed, transferred their corporate headquarters to Dallas, Texas. Dan was offered the opportunity to move with them, which he decided to accept because it would be a good career move. The decision to move to another state so far away was not without struggle; he was concerned about leaving me alone with no family in south Florida. I was touched by his concern but assured him I was not old and infirm yet and was still able to take care of myself. Because Dan would have been without a job had he not taken the opportunity offered him, I encouraged him to do what he thought was best for him and his career and not base his decision on whether he should leave me. So Dan and Scott, his new and last partner as of this writing, moved to Dallas.

The next year, the National Association of Church Business Administration (of which I was a member) held its conference in Dallas, which afforded me the longed-for opportunity to visit my son. This also raised an issue I had not yet had to face. Would it be appropriate for me to spend the night at Dan and Scott's apartment? Or would that send a signal that I was weakening in my stand against the wrongness of Dan's relationship with Scott? Would my spending the night there somehow communicate tacit approval of their sleeping arrangements? I could not decide the answer to this question on the basis of whether I would feel uncomfortable spending the night in their apartment; rather, I wanted to know what God wanted me to do in this situation. Is this something he would approve? Once again, I needed to go to the Lord and his Word to find some answers.

I went back to the Gospels to see if I could find out what Jesus might have done in a comparable situation. Interestingly, I discovered that the record of Jesus going to dinner at the home of Matthew, the tax collector, and having dinner with *many* tax collectors and sinners is chronicled not once but in three of the Gospels (Matthew 9:10-13, Mark 2:15-17, and Luke 5:27-31). Mark 2:15 even records that *many* tax collectors and sinners were followers of Jesus. What was even more interesting was the condemning attitude of the Pharisees, the Jewish religious leaders of Jesus' day, and Jesus' response to them. In each recorded instance, the Pharisees showed their disapproval and condemnation of Jesus for this action by questioning his disciples, "Why does your teacher eat with tax collectors and sinners?"

But it was Jesus who, overhearing their question, answered them, "It is not the healthy who need a doctor, but the sick. I have not come to call the righteous but sinners to repentance."

The self-righteous Pharisees readily acknowledged the sinfulness of others whom society viewed with disdain but could not see their own sinfulness and need of repentance. However, the tax collectors and sinners eagerly desired to hear Jesus and felt welcome in his presence. Luke 15:1-2 tells us that the "tax collectors and sinners were *all gathering around to hear Jesus.*" But the Pharisees and the teachers of the law muttered, "This man *welcomes* sinners and eats with them" (emphasis added).

In Luke 7:34, Jesus quotes what the Pharisees have said about him; they called him a "friend of sinners." I suspect Jesus may have taken that as a compliment and worn the title as a badge of honor!

These recorded attitudes and actions of Jesus assured me that it would not be wrong or inappropriate for me to spend the night at Dan's apartment. I must admit, though, that when it was time to go to bed that night I had to ask God for help to enable me to intentionally set my mind on other things and not on what might be going on in *their* bedroom. I have continued to feel free to stay in their home, whether in Texas, California (where they moved next), or in Florida when they later moved back there. I have prayed each time that my presence would be a blessing to them, and that I would rely on the life of Christ within me to relax and be natural and comfortable in their home. In turn, they have always been gracious and respectful to me and made me feel very welcome.

This also showed me that other situations would arise that would require me to determine the right response and course of action. For each situation, it was critically important to seek the Lord for guidance from his Word and by his Spirit and not make decisions based only on my own comfort or discomfort level or the opinion of others.

During my first visit, Scott seemed a little reserved and perhaps uncomfortable around me, but I kept praying that he could see I did love and accept him as a person, even if I could not accept his and Dan's relationship. Now, after a number of subsequent visits in their home, Scott makes me feel very welcome and greets me warmly when I arrive. On my part, I have come to recognize and appreciate Scott not only as a person but also as a gifted and creative designer whose talents are evident in the way he tastefully decorates their home.

Dan and Scott have, at this writing, been together for over seventeen years and, according to my son, have a mutually loving, monogamous relationship. I have come to recognize they are not just sexual partners, they are also friends, and I understand they genuinely care for one another. While I am thankful their relationship is harmonious and not destructive or violent as some homosexual relationships are, I still grieve over the wrong and sinful aspect of their relationship. As Robert Gagnon points out, "Positive moral conduct in many areas of one's life does not establish the legitimacy of all of one's conduct."[8]

The Lord has made it possible for me to have a good relationship with each of Dan's partners (with the possible exception of Andrew—likable, but not trustworthy), but I realize I have been spared what could have been much more difficult and complex situations because none of his partners were extremely challenging to love. They were likable young men, and none of them were out on the far end of the spectrum of extreme homosexuality or, to my knowledge, involved in substance abuse.

I am also aware that the situation of other parents may be quite different. But I believe there are some general principles that can be applied to any partner situation:

- Be willing to be obedient to God's Word regarding loving others, especially those who seem harder to love, or at least be open and willing for God to enable you to love them with his love. This may take some time, but God always honors obedience, and if you are willing, he will provide his grace to enable you to be obedient in this situation.

- See the partner as someone God loves, no matter where they may be on the broad homosexual spectrum or how difficult they may be from a human perspective to love.

- Much depends on the position of your loved one in regard to the partner. Does he or she want you to meet and accept the partner? If so, express your willingness (if you are at that point) to do so. If your loved one is hesitant for you to meet the partner, don't force the issue. You can be praying for the partner without ever meeting him or her. If your child is insistent upon your immediate acceptance of his or her partner but you are not at that point yet, be honest and explain that this situation is very difficult for you and that you need some time to emotionally and mentally work through it. Tell your child you are trying to get to that place and that hopefully you will be ready and able to meet the partner in a loving and gracious way in the near future.

- Some difficult situations may be forestalled if from the very beginning it is made clear to your loved one that you will continue to love him or her in spite of his or her immoral behavior, but you cannot and will not compromise the moral convictions and principles of the Bible. In a kind but firm way, make your position known and that you expect your loved one to respect it even if he or she doesn't agree with it.

- Clarify that some situations are nonnegotiable. If your child lives in another city or state and wants to bring the partner when coming to visit you, welcome the partner if you can genuinely do so, but make it clear they cannot sleep together or occupy the same bedroom in your home and that this stipulation would be the same if his or her partner was of the opposite sex.

- Pray about every situation that you face on this new journey. Pray for your child, for the partner, and for whatever relationship you may be able to have with him or her. Pray for God's direction and leading as you reach out in love to the partner. Don't be too sensitive to a negative response from the partner, and be ready to extend forgiveness for any rejection or wounding the partner may project toward you. We really don't have an "out" on this. God's Word is very clear. We are to forgive even our enemies.

> But I tell you: Love your enemies and pray for those who persecute you. (Matthew 5:44)

> But love your enemies, do good to them. (Luke 6:35)

- Loving and forgiving one's enemy or those who come against us and confronting wrongdoing are not incompatible responses. As we depend on him, God can show us how and when we need to confront wrong actions or attitudes and when it is time and appropriate to extend compassion, grace, and forgiveness to the wrongdoer.

- Intentionally prioritize time to spend in God's Word. Through his Word, God can provide knowledge, direction, encouragement, awareness of his promises, and—perhaps most importantly—hope. He can also by his Spirit change our own hearts to more accurately reflect his heart in interactions with a loved one's partners. God does not intend for you to walk this journey alone. He has promised to go before you and be with you. "The LORD himself goes before you and will be with you; he will never leave you nor forsake you. Do not be afraid; do not be discouraged" (Deuteronomy 31:8).

Understandably, as the mother of a gay-identified son, I have written about the relationship of partners primarily from the perspective of male homosexual relationships, but much of the material, and the above principles in particular, applies to both male and female homosexual partners. However, as addressed in chapter eight, there are some unique differences in lesbian relationships— primarily the stronger emotional element and higher incidence of short-term relationships.

This lengthy chapter must come to an end, but the subject of partners is not really complete without telling the rest of the story about John Michael, Dan's former partner. It cannot be omitted, because it is a striking reminder of the vital importance of being obedient when God calls us to love the partner of our homosexual child. The rest of John Michael's story will be told at the conclusion of the next chapter.

Chapter 13

Change: A Possibility? A Reality?

For as long as my son could remember, he had felt different from other boys; as a young boy, he more easily identified with girls and their activities than other boys and their rough and tumble ways. But as he entered puberty, to his dismay and further confusion, he discovered he was physically attracted to boys, not girls. He didn't choose to be that way, he just was. He didn't know why, but somehow things had become reversed from what they should have been. His painful conclusion: He must be gay, was born that way, and change was not possible. This conclusion, though faulty, was strengthened by what he heard from the gay community: "Once gay, always gay." But I was not ready to accept that as a foregone conclusion. I thought there must be some way he could be "fixed."

Like me, most parents who find themselves in a similar situation are not ready to accept the oft-repeated dogma from the current culture: "Born gay—can't change." They want hope that change is possible. They want an easy and quick fix to make their child "normal" again. Surely there must be a counselor we can send our loved one to who will be able to change him or her back to "normal." But I, like other parents, soon learned I couldn't fix Dan. There was no magic pill that would change or eliminate all his same-sex attractions and desires. As much as I wanted to find it, I had to finally conclude there was no prescribed formula to follow that would guarantee an instantaneous or even gradual change from homosexual to heterosexual. But that did not mean change was not possible. What I did learn was that although change is complicated, involved, and not easy, it is possible. And therein lay hope.

The Possibility of Change

The first question to consider is basic: What is your loved one's level of involvement in homosexuality? In his brochure, "The Ten Myths of Homosexuality," under "Myth No. 2: Sexual orientation can never change," Peter Sprigg points out the importance of clarifying three different phenomena that fall under the umbrella term of *sexual orientation*:

- a person's sexual attractions or desires
- a person's sexual behavior
- a person's self-identification, either publicly or internally ("gay" or "lesbian," or increasingly in today's homosexual-supporting culture—"bisexual.")[1]

It is easy to assume that because someone has same-sex attractions that automatically means they are engaging in same-sex relationships and have identified themselves as gay, but that is not necessarily the case. Interestingly, as I was writing this chapter, there was an article in the daily newspaper about a Lutheran pastor in Minneapolis who publicly opposes homosexuals being allowed to lead congregations. His own sexuality had become an issue after a gay magazine reported his membership in a support group for Christians battling same-sex attractions and accused him of being a hypocrite. When interviewed by the Associated Press, the minister readily admitted that he has known for many years that he is attracted to men, but he does not consider himself a hypocrite because he is still a virgin at age fifty-seven. He does not identify himself as gay because he has never acted on his urges. I personally know other men who have struggled with same-sex attractions but have never acted on them. Research substantiates this reality.[2]

If your loved one is struggling with unwanted same-sex attractions and desires but has never moved past that to homosexual behavior, his or her disclosure may be a cry for help. It is important for a parent to understand the involuntary nature of homosexual attractions. Your loved one did not *choose* to have those attractions. Rather, he or she *discovered* the attractions were there. If this is where your loved one is, he or she may well be very relieved to hear there is hope and help available. He or she may be very open to going to a good Christian counselor, trained and experienced in dealing with sexual disorders and especially homosexual issues, and may also be willing to join a Christian support group for people struggling with same-sex attractions if there is one in your vicinity.

A second basic question is, Is your loved one looking for help or wanting to change? Unless the teenager or young adult who has disclosed his or her gay identity or homosexual involvement wants help for his or her struggle and relief from the bondage of homosexuality, a parent's options are more limited. You cannot make that decision for your child.

Your son or daughter may believe they have found their true identity, and embracing it has become a way to resolve the conflicted feelings and desires he or she have struggled with for as long as he or she can remember. Forming relationships with other gay-identified people may have given him or her a sense of community, of finding others like him- or herself who understand and accept him or her. He or she may merely be at the point where he or she wants to come out and no longer hide what he or she believes is his or her true identity, especially from his or her parents. He or she is not looking to change but are hoping you will still love and accept him or her.

I remember one early conversation I had with my son. As I began to read and accumulate information on homosexuality, I was anxious to share some of what I was learning with him. But when I broached the subject, he quickly let me know he was not interested in hearing it.

Puzzled by his response, I pleaded with him. "Honey, I'm only trying to give you hope."

He promptly replied, "I don't want hope! I don't want to change! I'm happy being gay!"

As difficult as it was for me to accept, I had to acknowledge change would not come for Dan through his mother's persuasive words or attempting to force on him all my newly acquired information and insights on homosexuality. "Change" for Dan was not something that could come from me. It had to begin with his *wanting* to change and accepting the possibility of change.

Nevertheless, let's establish the evidence for the possibility of change. This is critical because the stance promoted by pro-homosexual advocates is that homosexuality is immutable—a person's sexual orientation was already determined at birth and cannot be changed. They counter the claims of change by others with the argument that the person wasn't really a homosexual to begin with. He or she was actually a heterosexual who was temporarily engaging or experimenting in homosexual behavior. Or they allege that if he or she is truly gay, he or she will eventually go back to his or her homosexual friends and practices.

In the battle to redefine marriage and legalize gay marriage, which is argued more and more in the courts and even made legal in some states, immutability is a key element of the argument presented by the homosexual lobby. They claim, therefore, those who oppose homosexuality or the legalization of gay marriage are being intolerant and unloving, denying homosexuals their civil rights and treating them much like African Americans were treated for decades.

An interesting sidebar at this point is to note that the pro-gay lobby's claim of immutability is one of the things that upsets people in the African American community. Crystal Dixon, former administrator at the University of Toledo, who was fired from her position as assistant vice president of human resources for her stance against homosexual practices, brings clarity to that issue. She wrote in a column for the Toledo Free Press:

As a Black woman, I take great umbrage at the notion that those choosing the homosexual lifestyle are "civil rights victims." Here's why. I cannot wake up tomorrow and not be a Black woman. I am genetically and biologically a Black woman and very pleased to be so as my Creator intended.[3]

The pro-gay advocates are angered by those who claim that change is possible because it refutes the "born gay" position and thereby invalidates their claim that this is a civil rights issue. "Change" disproves their immutability assertion.

Though it must be emphasized that homosexual *attractions* are clearly *not* a choice while consensual homosexual *conduct is* a choice, research increasingly shows that a change in both behavior *and* attractions is possible. A person's internal sexual desires or attractions are undoubtedly the most difficult aspect of sexual orientation to change, but evidence demonstrates that many people have experienced change in that way as well. Peter Sprigg shares the following:

> One of the strongest pieces of evidence for the possibility of change comes from an unlikely source—Dr. Robert Spitzer, a psychiatrist who was instrumental in the pivotal 1973 decision of the American Psychiatric Association to remove homosexuality from its official list of mental disorders. Spitzer studied 200 people who had reported some measure of change from a homosexual to a heterosexual orientation as a result of what is sometimes called "reparative therapy" for unwanted same-sex attractions. He concluded, "The changes following reparative therapy were not limited to sexual behavior and sexual orientation self-identity. The changes encompassed sexual attraction, arousal, fantasy, yearning, and being bothered by homosexual feelings. The changes encompassed the core aspects of sexual orientation."[4]

Another study referenced by Sprigg gives further credibility to the possibility of change. "A survey of over 800 individuals who had participated in a variety of efforts to change from a homosexual orientation found that 34.3% had shifted 'to an exclusively or almost exclusively heterosexual orientation."[5]

A more recent study released in 2009 by psychologists Stanton L. Jones of Wheaton College and Mark A. Yarhouse of Regent University is a follow-up to a study released two years earlier in the form of a book, *Ex-Gays?* The first study was considered groundbreaking, and the follow-up study was no less significant. The seven-year study followed sixty-one subjects who were going through programs set up by Exodus International, a former Christian ministry that sought to help those who wanted to leave homosexuality. It is important to note that although Exodus funded the study, Jones and Yarhouse agreed to conduct it only if all sides agreed that they would report the results no matter the outcome—in other words, even if the findings embarrassed Exodus!

Here are some of their findings:

- 23 percent reported a successful conversion to heterosexual attractions.
- 30 percent reported living a celibate life and were content with their reduction in homosexual attractions. These two categories were combined by the researchers for a 53 percent success rate.
- 16 percent of subjects had modest decreases in homosexual attractions and weren't satisfied with their degree of change but were committed to continuing the process.
- 7 percent had seen no decrease in homosexual attractions but had not given up trying to change.
- 25 percent of subjects were considered "failures," either because they gave up on the process and once again identified themselves as homosexual (20 percent) or because they had not yet embraced a homosexual identity but nevertheless had given up [on the change effort] (5 percent).

Jones emphasized that the best way to test whether change is possible is to "study people as they are attempting change, and follow them over a period of time. Our study found that a significant portion of that population reported very significant change."[6]

Reality of Change

But perhaps the best and most convincing evidence of not only the possibility but the reality of change are the testimonies of individuals who have actually experienced lasting change over a period of time.

Christine Sneeringer

From the time she was very young, Christine resisted looking like a girl. She thought girls were weak and if men viewed her as pretty, they would see her as a prospective victim. But to Christine, boys were strong, so outwardly she did everything she could to be viewed as a boy. She kept her hair cut short, walked like a boy, talked like a boy, dressed like a boy, and even spit like a boy! The proof of her success in this effort was that she was often mistaken as a boy and addressed by adults as "son" or "young man" and was even scolded for being in women's public restrooms. She insisted her family and friends call her "Chris" because the shorter version of her name could also be considered masculine.

Christine's concept of womanhood was negatively shaped very early in her home as she watched her alcoholic father verbally and physically abuse her mother. Even though the father took the family to church, at home he took Bible verses out of context, using them to exert his authority and demand absolute submission from his wife. What this communicated to Christine was two distinct impressions: Women are weak, passive, and defenseless, and God does not think very highly of women; therefore, Christianity had nothing to offer her.

Also forming in Christine's mind was a deep mistrust and negative view of men. This perception was enforced when, at the age of twelve, she was molested more than once by an older male relative. Following her parents' divorce, she and her sister were sent to another state to live with relatives for a year. Since these were not her parents, she believed she could not tell anyone about the abuse she was enduring. Her confusion, shame, and distorted sense of blame only added to her conviction that it was not safe to be a girl. To Christine, being a girl was a liability. If being pretty meant that guys would find her attractive, she did not want that because men could not be trusted.

Being a troubled teenager did not keep Christine from making good grades and excelling in sports, but she exhibited behavioral problems at school. Not understanding her own deep, unfilled need for attention, affection, and affirmation, Christine found herself attracted to an older teenage girl who also was a top athlete. Their friendship was strong and intense and filled a deep emotional need in Christine's life. When she unexpectedly learned that her new friend was gay, she followed the advice of a trusted older woman friend who encouraged her to pursue a romantic relationship with Katie. This was the beginning of several lesbian relationships that even included an older married woman.

In her early twenties, Christine had given up on being straight and had also given up on God after a brief involvement in a controlling, cult-like group at college. But God had not given up on Christine. God used her passion for sports to draw Christine to join a women's church softball team. Despite her bad language and unsportsmanlike attitude—very unsuited for a church-sponsored team—the Christian coach did not correct Christine for her bad behavior. Instead, he saw this as an opportunity to reach out to Christine with Christlike kindness and told her teammates to love and pray for her. Later, referring back to that time, Christine said, "If I had known they were praying for me, I would have told them to stop. In my arrogance, I thought I knew what I needed to be happy. I had a lesbian lover and was content with my life. But God was pursuing me through this experience."

In time, Christine was drawn to the peace and love she saw in her teammates and began attending some of the church services because she wanted to know more about the God they were serving. She began meeting with Kelly, one of her softball teammates, for weekly Bible study. During that time, Christine made a profession of faith, deciding she wanted God even more than she wanted her homosexuality. Her newfound faith did not immediately take away her homosexual feelings, but it put her on a path of growth in God, which was the first step in her journey out. Kelly continued to disciple and support her through the difficult decision to sever all ties with her lover.

God persisted in directing Christine's path and brought her into contact with a ministry that helped her understand the roots of her lesbianism in light of her childhood circumstances. Through her contact with a support group, individual counseling, and regular involvement in a strong, Bible-teaching church, Christine began developing strong, healthy, same-sex relationships, which she says was a pivotal factor in her healing.

One major obstacle for Christine to overcome in her journey was her negative body image and view of femininity. Years of looking and acting masculine had left her uncertain of what it means to be a woman, and she struggled with many insecurities. But God was still directing her steps, and while attending her first conference for those struggling with same-sex attractions, Christine experienced a total makeover that helped her see herself in a new light. After a new hairstyle, manicure, artful makeup application, and color consultation, Christine was overwhelmed with emotion at the revelation that she had the potential to be pretty just like all the other girls at church she admired and wanted to fit in with.

The outer transformation helped Christine feel more comfortable presenting a feminine face to the world, but she knew that makeup does not heal a lesbian. It was only the outward evidence of an inward change, allowing her to embrace a feminine identity without feeling threatened. Her testimony is, "I'm finally embracing what God meant me to be. I'm changed from the inside out. Being a woman isn't a liability anymore . . . and that's truly beautiful!"[7]

As mentioned earlier in this book, Christine has walked in freedom from lesbianism since 1990 and became the director of Worthy Creations in 1999. She speaks regularly at conferences and workshops, both nationally and internationally. She is frequently interviewed on radio and TV, and her story has been featured in a number of magazines. Her passion is to share the transforming work of Christ in her own life and help others who are seeking freedom from homosexuality.

Willy Torresin de Oliveira

Willy grew up in a religious family and attended church each Sunday with his family. But daily home life was another story. His father had a serious drinking problem and kept losing one job after another. His mother tried to compensate by working outside the home and trying to fill the roles of both mother and father. Somehow in those early years of his life, Willy got the message that he had to be good to be loved and accepted by his parents, particularly his father.

The impression formed early in his mind was that love was based on his behavior and performance. Sadly, this thinking also influenced his concept of God; God would love him only if he did not sin. So he resolved he would not sin so God would love him.

In those days, no one spoke openly about sexuality, but the implicit message was that anything to do with sex was wrong and sinful. This view was intensified when he was sexually molested by an adult woman when he was only five or six. Early in his teenage years, Willy begin feeling there was something wrong with him, something that had to do with his sexuality, but he did not know what it was.

In his teen years, looking for a refuge from his stormy home life and also wanting to please God by being good and doing the right things, Willy became more and more involved in church activities.

At the age of eighteen, he followed the suggestion of some pastors in his church and enrolled in seminary to become a pastor. Still trying to earn God's approval, he also became involved in missionary work.

But he was also becoming increasingly aware that something was wrong in his sexuality, so he began reading books on sexuality where he came across a description of same-sex attraction. Much to his horror, he had to admit to himself that he was struggling with homosexual feelings and desires. At that time, he believed that homosexual practice was the worst possible sin, and that people who struggled with and practiced those things would be totally rejected by God. So he promised himself—and God—that he would never do those things. To protect himself, he avoided friendships with men; he felt safer befriending girls or just being alone as he had always been all his life.

One day, three young men came to him and said, "We're gay. Do you think God can change us?"

Willy was startled by their question but quickly answered matter-of-factly, "Of course. Nothing is impossible with God." But his heart sank in despair, for he was painfully aware that although he had been praying, fasting, reading the Bible, memorizing Scriptures, and doing everything he could to be a "good" Christian, his feelings and attractions toward other men were increasing, not diminishing.

Willy decided to talk to his supervisor in the missionary work. It was very hard to open up with anyone about his personal problems, but he felt it was the only thing he could do at that time. However, his leader didn't offer any help at all; instead, he sent Willy back home.

Disillusioned, he left missionary work but continued his involvement in church activities. He felt confused and alone. He wanted to talk to someone but was afraid of being rejected again, so he kept his struggle a secret. One day, he attended a missionary conference and, ironically, had his first sexual encounter with another male seminary student. Strangely, the sexual part of the encounter had not been the most important for him; he wanted to be embraced again and told he was loved. He was hungry for more affection and emotional involvement with another man.

At that time, Willy made the crucial decision to go to a gay bar and was surprised by how free he felt there. For the first time in his life, he felt could be himself and not hide behind a mask. It was like heaven on earth to him. From that day on, he stopped going to church and ended all his involvement in religious activities. There were times when deep within he felt disturbed, but he tried to quiet those inner feelings by surrounding himself with friends and drinking more.

Gradually, all Willy's devotion and desire to serve God turned to rebellion and anger. He was tired of trying to please a God whom he obviously could not please, so he gave up trying. Besides, he believed he had committed the unpardonable sin, and that there was no hope for him and he could not find his way back to God.

Willy spent about fifteen years of his life trying to find purpose and meaning in a long-lasting relationship with another man. But after the end of several long-term relationships, he realized he was not finding any solutions or answers to his deep, inner longings. He also realized he no longer *wanted* or believed in a long-term relationship with another man. He grew increasingly frustrated and depressed.

Although Willy had given up on God, God had not given up on Willy and began pursuing him by unexpectedly and tenderly saying to him, "I love you." The words were very clear, but Willy had no idea where they were coming from. Was it all just in his mind? Although he suspected whose words they were, he could not believe it was really God. He was so deep in sin; how could God possibly love him? But once in a while, unexpectedly he would hear the words again. "I love you, my son, and I have so much for you."

Things came to a head one Saturday afternoon when Willy was outside his house washing his car and heard the voice again. This time, Willy reacted in anger. He threw down the bucket of water and stormed into the house and down to the basement where he could vent his stored up anger at God. He screamed out at God, "Don't you have anything else to do? Leave me alone! Stop doing this to me! I can't serve you! I tried all I could to do the things you wanted me to do, to become the person you wanted me to be, but I failed! Why don't you leave me alone? I know there's no hope for me! You made me this way, didn't you? Aren't you happy? Leave me alone!"

When Willy was finished shouting at God, he fully expected God to open the ground under his feet and send him directly to hell. But instead, he heard these gentle words, "Are you through?" When Willy had nothing more to say, God continued, "Do you think you have anything I need? Do you think I need your money, your time, your work? Do you think I need you at all? When did I ask you to do all those things?"

Willy was stunned. "But God, I always heard people in church telling me this is what I ought to be doing—"

"Why didn't you ask *me* what I really wanted from you?"

Willy had no answer. He realized he had never asked God what *he* wanted. "God, what is it then that you want from me?"

"I want your heart."

"What do you want my heart for? It is so filthy! It is filled with sin. And worse, sins that I love, that have become part of my life. What are you going to do with this filthy heart of mine?"

"I'm going to pour my life into it."

"But why?"

"Because that's what I made you for—to pour my life into you! And because I love you. Will you accept my love?"

Those words somehow satisfied the hunger and thirst for love and significance that Willy had been trying so hard to meet through other men without success. Deep inside, Willy thought, *This is it, this is what I have been looking for!* Yet he felt he could never measure up and deserve God's love or even be able to change his life to match what he thought God would expect from him. He said to God, "I can't change my life. I can't give up on my boyfriend. I can't go back to a church again. I can't do anything for you."

He was surprised when God answered, "I'm not asking you to give me anything or do anything for me. I'm offering *you* something. Will you accept my love? I don't want anything in return."

Willy could not believe it. It sounded too good to be true. Although he hesitated, something inside him screamed for that love. "God, if you want to just love me, without asking me for anything, I accept it. I accept your love."

At that point, Willy was literally flooded with God's love in a way he could not explain. He just felt loved by God in a way that he never dreamed was possible, and it had absolutely nothing to do with anything he could offer God in return. The depth of God's love was overwhelming, and Willy let himself just bask in that love. For the first time, his life had a purpose. It all made sense; this was what he was created for, to experience this love, this awesome God. At first, it all felt too good to be true, but then that feeling was replaced by a more certain one. "This is *so good,* and *it is true!*"

The emotional aspect of Willy's dramatic encounter with God in time did decrease, but the experience and reality of God's love did not. Because of the intense reality of his encounter with God, there was a new desire in his heart not only to know God in a deeper way but also to *be* like God. Willy was finding in God all that he had been looking for in homosexual practice all those years, and homosexual practice began to lose its attractiveness to him. Willy took the initiative to end the relationship he was in and asked God to remove his homosexual identity and practices and also the sexual addictions from his life. As he made these decisions, he discovered God's love and grace were available to him to walk this new life— step-by-step and day by day.

A number of years have now passed since these changes took place in Willy's life. He has learned to respond to the pain of his wounds in nonsexual ways and has been healed of many of those wounds. He has learned to turn to God when he is tempted and trust him for all his needs.

Willy now has a deep desire in his heart to share this amazing and transforming love of God with others—to proclaim the gospel of God's love, grace, and peace to anyone who will listen, but particularly to those who feel trapped in homosexuality as he was. They need to know there is no sin God cannot forgive and no bondage that he cannot break.

Today Willy is back at the church of his childhood, where he is a missionary and also involved in teaching. He is the founder and director of a ministry called "Peace with God," based on Romans 5:1, providing counseling and discipleship to people who desire to understand who they are in Christ and how God redeems their sexuality.[8]

As Willy shared his testimony with me to use in this chapter, he made this pertinent comment, "This all happened in 1996, and it is as true as if it were happening right now. It doesn't get old!"

Edward and Jessica, husband and wife

Edward

"And you know where you're headed!" she exclaimed with tears in her eyes, as she pointed downward. I knew she meant hell. She was hurt, visibly upset, and shocked at the words I had uttered earlier, "Mom, I'm gay." I was twenty-one and chose to tell her in the kitchen as I helped with the dishes. She kept asking me why I had broken off the two-year relationship with my girlfriend that seemed to be going so well. When I finally told her, she responded, "I knew it. I knew something was up."

It quickly spiraled into an emotional exchange. "I've always tried to be a good son," I remember saying at one point.

"And? What does that have to do with this?" she asked. Subconsciously, I was trying to make up for the day this would happen—the day I would let down my parents. When things had settled a bit, she warned, "Don't tell your father. Let me do it."

My father was a handsome man who enjoyed wearing suits and plenty of cologne à la Ricky Ricardo. Divorced from his first wife, he was mayor of a small, sugar mill industry town in Cuba. My mother, who was very smart, came from a well-to-do family who lived in that town and attended the Presbyterian church there. Against her pastor's and parents' wishes, she married the divorced mayor, and together they fled communist Cuba in 1961 and sought political asylum in the United States, where my three siblings and I were born.

At the age of two, I was molested by an older cousin. I cannot say with certainty that this incident triggered my homosexual attractions, but it certainly exposed me to a sexual act with another male at a very tender age. As a child, I loved the arts. I also loved superheroes and, accompanied by a vivid imagination, acted out the roles of TV characters. One minute I was Steve Austin with bionic limbs, and the next, I was Diana Prince with a magic lasso.

My mother celebrated my art and boasted of my talent to her friends and family, but my father was indifferent about it and at times preferred my older brother to me. I vividly recall when he began taking my brother to work with him in the summers. My father benefited from a helping hand, and my brother was happy for a summer job. He was thirteen, so he could actually help some. I was only ten, more of a liability than anything else, but this was never explained to me. I would hang onto the car door, crying and begging to go with them, eventually watching as the men drove off and I was left behind with my mother and two sisters, with whom I developed close relationships. I picked up their mannerisms and phrases, which became obvious to other boys who soon labeled me "sissy," "faggot," "queer," and the like.

Dad was a hard worker who fulfilled his duty as a provider for the family; however, his duty as a caring, loving father lacked when he drank, which he did frequently. I remember being terrified when he was drunk. My mother would go into survival mode, pouring her fears and insecurities into her children and sharing intimate details too heavy for my young shoulders to bear. Of course, at that age, I did not realize how incredibly unhealthy this was. All I knew was my father was bad and my mother was good. I recall making a conscious decision not to be anything like my father. Sadly, he represented heterosexuality and everything male to me. I detached from my father emotionally as I did from the bullies at school, but inside—way deep inside—I wanted to belong. But I felt ill-equipped, damaged, and different.

When I was thirteen and finally old enough to help my father in the summers, we often would stop at his friend's barbershop where he would begin a long night of drinking with his buddies. The shop had stacks and stacks of pornographic magazines that I was allowed to peruse. I found myself drawn to the male figures. For hours, nearly every time we would visit, I viewed all the porn I wanted. Once again, this might not be the reason I developed same-sex attractions, but it exposed me to sexuality at a very young age.

My parents divorced when I was fourteen. My mother was back in school, learning to speak English, and drove a cool Pontiac Firebird. At an age when most teenage boys look up to their fathers, my hero was my mother. My parents remarried after my father sobered up. He never drank again and even tried reaching out to me, but I was cold and distant.

At fifteen, I had my first gay experience with a senior in high school. Ironically, the girl who willingly introduced us quickly informed me soon after that it was a sin. I had attended the local Baptist church enough to know what sin was and stopped immediately. I started attending a Lutheran church and, as God would have it, my first night there a man was being reconciled to the church and his family after having abandoned both for a gay life two years earlier. I received Christ as my Savior at that church and began praying for my family. One by one, they were all saved, and we became very involved in the church.

In my early twenties, I realized that my same-sex attractions were still very much present. I allowed myself to fantasize, which of course created an even bigger appetite. I prayed for God to take it all away. I even had a girlfriend, but by the time I entered college, I had started experimenting with other guys and quickly broke off the relationship. This was the breakup my mother was so curious about at the beginning of my story. She could not understand how the son who led them all to Christ was now declaring he was gay.

In college, I met other men and women who claimed to be gay and Christian. I began wondering, questioning, and compromising and finally decided to see for myself what it was all about. After all, I believed in Jesus and was a Christian. If I was having these desires, perhaps God *did* make me this way, so perhaps it was not a sin after all. Sadly, what was going to be an experiment lasted twelve years. By my mid-thirties, I was living in New York City—acting and designing, with a partner, a house, and cars. Yet something was missing. Something wasn't right. During the twelve years I was in the gay life, I never opened a Bible or darkened the entrance of a church. I would pray quickly at night to avoid listening to God. Then 9/11 occurred.

Strange things were happening in the world around me. I had a weird feeling that a line was being drawn in the sand, urging me to decide whether I was truly a follower of Christ. My partner was away on an acting gig for two months, so I had plenty of time to think and work on the house we had just purchased. Around that time, I started listening to a Florida preacher on Christian radio. In my time alone, I began feeling the heavy presence of the Holy Spirit; I knew he was drawing close. One day, in the midst of cleaning the bathroom, I felt his presence again. As he convicted me about the life I was living, I literally felt a tightening in my chest and finally dropped what I had in my hand. Tears welled up and I cried out loud, "Lord, I hear you! I know I say I'm a Christian, but I don't live like one. I've tried, but I can't change." But he was not asking me to change. He was asking me to come back!

I went online to search for Christians who had left the gay life and found story after story of people who had come out of the gay life through Jesus Christ. I began wrestling with God through prayer while pacing back and forth, full of questions. "Wasn't this love?"

Five days later, I surrendered. I found my old Bible and opened it for the first time in twelve years. I read, "Do not be deceived . . ." followed by a descriptive list of sins, including the practice of homosexuality, and a clear statement that persons who practice them will not enter the kingdom of heaven (1 Corinthians 6:9-10 ESV). But verse eleven filled my heart with hope: "Such *were* some of you . . ." (emphasis added). Scales dropped from my eyes. I fell to my knees and repented for all the years I had done things my way instead of his way. I did not know if I would ever be attracted to women or stop liking men; all I knew was that I wanted Jesus more than my sin. I wanted to be right with God again. That was August 22, 2002, and I have never looked back.

Soon after, I began attending a support group for Christians struggling with same-sex attractions. The counseling I received there was profound. They bathed me in prayer and the Word of God. When my partner returned from his acting gig, we broke up, and several months later, I returned home to a family who had never stopped praying for me. In previous visits with my partner, there were rules we followed at my parents' home, but my parents were always kind to my partners and—after the initial shock of my coming out—they were loving to me, despite my choice to pursue my attractions. This left an open door for reconciliation.

My return was wonderful. My family rejoiced in my rededication to Christ. I joined a support group and learned about the roots of homosexuality. I learned that my attractions/temptations might not be a choice but to act on them was. After awhile, I was encouraged to join a men's group at my church so I would not remain on the "ex-gay plateau." It was comforting to know others who struggled with similar issues, but recognizable healing occurred when God used other men with heterosexual backgrounds to disciple me. Those men affirmed me even when they did not understand my specific struggle because they knew what it was to struggle in other ways. Together, we all learned how to be better imitators of Christ and what it is to be a man of God. I began embracing my heterosexual identity and understanding my identity in Christ—not a homosexual trying to resolve my Christianity but, like others, a Christian who struggles with the flesh.

My father passed away in 2006, but not before we were reconciled. As my siblings and I cared for him in his last years, God revealed how resentful my heart still was toward him. I realized I had a choice: I could either remain angry or forgive as I was forgiven. In a hospital room in Miami, I released my father. In our broken past, my mother had painted a terrible picture of him in my young mind, but now God was using her to speak of my dad in edifying ways. "Your father loves you so much. Despite his Alzheimer's, he seems to remember you the most. Whenever you leave, if you don't give him a hug and a kiss, he becomes very sad." Her words were powerful and healing. My dad would hold my hand for long periods of time, tell me he loved me, and call me his boy. God did not have to do that for me, but he did. My view of my earthly father had affected my view of my heavenly Father, and he healed it.

I cannot remember exactly when I started noticing women in a very different light. They were organized, curvy, and beautiful—the perfect complement to forgetful, messy, and balding. For some reason, I was drawn to Wednesday night family dinners at our church. My single friends could not understand why I wanted to hang out with screaming kids, parents, and the elderly. But God was up to something. I began to appreciate kids and family, not as a bystander, but as someone who could possibly have a family of my own one day. God was stretching me, helping me grow into the man he intended me to be. In my gay life, I was childish and carefree, fleeing responsibility. As a man of God, I was facing challenges head-on with strength that only Jesus can provide. I allowed myself to go out as friends with a couple of Christian women from church and enjoyed it. One in particular whom I knew from support group was great. The more we went out, the more I wanted to see her. She loved Jesus, and I liked her. Within six months, we were going steady. Within a year, Jessica and I were married.

People ask me if I still have attractions to men. I suspect that as long as I am on this earth, I will experience the struggle between flesh and the Spirit. But what was once a mountain is now a molehill. I still experience temptation, but I handle it with God's Word, prayer, and accountability to other believers. The victories I have had in my progressive sanctification out of homosexuality have equipped me to handle other challenges, and my mind is constantly being transformed to deal with things God's way. He has blessed me with a wonderful wife, a ministry that helps others, and a new identity. To him be the glory!

Jessica

"God created man in His own image, in the image of God He created him; male and female He created them" (Genesis 1:27).

I was born and raised in Miami, Florida, by Cuban parents who were in their early twenties when they married and had me. When I was three, my parents divorced; subsequently, I lived with my mother and visited my father twice a week. Sadly, the teenage son of a caregiver molested me while I was a child, creating feelings of being trapped and unprotected that were to influence me for many years.

Living with a single mother who sought security in a series of relationships with men, two more of which resulted in marriage and divorce, I felt responsible for my mother's unhappiness, and that I needed to protect her from the hardships of life. Coping with these multiple family breakups strengthened my determination to be strong physically and emotionally. My mother looked up to me and viewed me as a confidante, and I assumed a leadership role in our home. Before long, we had reversed roles; I never felt like a daughter. My mother would vent her hardships and troubles, looking to me for strength and happiness.

Meanwhile, my father's unstable relationships with women also had a negative impact on me. He remarried but, some years later, divorced again, His lack of commitment contributed to my growing distrust of men and negative view of marriage. He also kept pornographic magazines easily accessible in his bathroom where I secretly looked at them and sexually fantasized about women during my preadolescent years.

The emotional and relational brokenness in both my mother's and father's homes distorted my understanding of how God created males and females in his image. I saw no hope in marriages or families. Being a woman was a weakness, and femininity was a deficit. I desperately wanted to "outgrow" being a girl.

I bonded with my father, enjoying boating, fishing, and sports with him and even adopting his masculine mannerisms, including his gait and posture. In my teens, my father admonished, "Looking that way, you'll never get a man in your life." I responded that I didn't want to look like a slut like other girls did just to get a boyfriend. I identified with my father's attitude of working hard at life, being strong, and striving for perfection in everything. The United States Army motto, "Be all you can be," so fittingly described me that in high school I was known as "GI Jessie." My attitude was very much a boot-camp approach to life, school, and sports.

At age ten, I began competing athletically and especially enjoyed contact sports like tae kwon do and soccer, but ballet was a year of torture. I never felt comfortable on the dance floor and could not identify with the other girls. Other sports, however, became my healthy outlet for the pressures of life. Throughout high school and college, I encountered teammates who were lesbians. While a freshman in college, I began to question my identity and sexuality, realizing that my curiosity about womanhood and attraction to other women had intensified. While in college, I began seeking friendships with girls who were gay-identified and learned more about their lifestyle. When a female basketball coach started giving me the attention I craved from another woman, the emotions grew and became sexualized, triggering my first experience in the gay lifestyle.

Growing up, I had been a devout Roman Catholic. While in college, I still practiced Catholic traditions but felt conflicted while receiving Holy Communion because I knew that, according to church teaching, acting out homosexually was a sexual sin. I suppressed these thoughts, however, after a priest told me it was okay to have those attractions, and that I just had a special way of loving.

Emotionally fractured from my parents' divorces, the relational brokenness of their homes, molestation as a child, and now spiritually,

I was even more confused. I tried dating guys and having sexual relationships with them to see if things would change but found myself more attracted to women. Resolving my sexual conflicts and identity was a higher priority than being religious, so, at age nineteen, I decided to accept who I was and began living openly as a gay-identified lesbian, a lifestyle that lasted for eight years.

A couple of years after college, the mother of my partner at the time began to have a big impact on me. A Christian, she treated me with kindness, showering me with the love of Christ. Despite my relationship with her daughter, she saw my need for a relationship with Jesus. With grace, she shared the truth of Christ and one day invited me to church. Though intimidated and totally unfamiliar with an evangelical Protestant church, I nevertheless trusted her and agreed to go.

There I experienced the awesome presence of the Lord, hearing the Word of God like never before. Afterward, I had a lot of questions and again felt conflicted; I told my partner's mother I was sorry for violating a house that honors the Lord, but I truly loved her daughter and didn't know any other way to live except the gay lifestyle. The woman told me that Jesus loves me and encouraged me to trust him with my life but said that his commandments to his followers would mean severing all ties with ungodly things of this world, including homosexuality. At this point, I believed in Jesus but did not know how to trust him. I hungered to learn more about Jesus and the Bible.

Eventually, my relationship with the woman's daughter ended. A few months later, a job opportunity opened up in Miami, and I moved back to south Florida. Although I had not accepted Jesus as Lord and Savior and was not ready to leave the gay lifestyle, I made it a priority to find a church that worshipped Jesus and taught the Bible.

I began attending a Baptist church weekly, and after about eight months, a guy from the church asked me out on a date. I declined and told him I was a lesbian. Despite my response, he continued demonstrating kindness and a caring, Christlike attitude toward me. Both he and the church's pastor later told me about a support group in Fort Lauderdale called Worthy Creations.

On May 22, 2000, I attended my first meeting, after which the ministry director immediately gave me two assignments. "You need to watch this Sy Rogers video and sign up for the Exodus Freedom Conference in San Diego, California." Though feeling overwhelmed with all the information, I nonetheless watched Sy's video that same evening. After hearing his powerful testimony, I wanted to have the same victory in Jesus. Alone in my apartment, I got on my knees, repented, and asked Jesus to be my Lord and Savior. Wanting to publicly affirm this important decision, I met with my pastor two days later after the midweek service and told him all that had happened, proclaiming I was now a new creation in Jesus Christ, wanted to be baptized on Sunday, and needed financial support to attend the Exodus conference that summer.

During the next three years, my understanding of my struggle with homosexuality grew as did my knowledge about its roots in my life. However, pride and self-righteousness also began sprouting in my heart, prompting me to phase out attendance at support group meetings. I continued attending church but avoided being with other women who would hold me accountable, instead counting on my own strength and ability to handle life. During this time, I enjoyed a new desire to date men but had several relationships with Christian men who also were sexually broken. One tried to force himself on me, and another broke off our relationship after dating a few months.

These experiences of rejection, abandonment, and abuse made me very vulnerable. I felt weak but told myself to be strong and move on with life. However, without Christians holding me accountable and still maintaining ungodly friendships, the desire to associate with gay friends and be loved and accepted in familiar surroundings was overwhelming. I soon returned to the gay lifestyle and entered into another lesbian relationship, which lasted two years.

This was the most painful thing I had yet experienced because I knew what the Word of God said yet wanted my sin more. I felt like a loser, a quitter, and a failure. I would berate myself, "How could I have fallen? I knew better. I should have been stronger!" I felt like God was keeping statistics on my behavior and my relationship with him. I started believing that I had lost my salvation because my attraction to women had grown stronger again. Eventually, I began abusing drugs and alcohol to numb the pain of the guilt and shame. I felt like my life was over.

But God was bigger than my pain. He showed me what true love is; he didn't walk away or divorce me. I clearly recalled his words, "I will never leave thee or forsake thee" (Hebrews 13:5 KJV). The Holy Spirit within me reminded me of God's Word and promises. "Behold, the LORD's hand is not so short that it cannot save; nor is His ear so dull that it cannot hear. But your iniquities have made a separation between you and your God" (Isaiah 59:1-2 NASB).

Again, I was convicted of my sin and repented. God reminded me of the promise in Philippians 1:6 that he would complete what he had begun in my life. I realized I didn't have to start at mile zero of the journey, but I did need to acknowledge him as God, die to self, and pick up my cross as I followed him by faith. I asked God to help, and he reached out and pulled me up, assuring me he would heal and redeem my wounds of rejection and abandonment.

After rededicating my life to Christ in 2006, I humbly went back to the support group and began to meet weekly with a Christian counselor. This time, I purposely sought help from my pastor and his wife and willfully made myself accountable to several mature Christian women in my church. Additionally, as a commitment to my restoration, I started a Living Waters discipleship ministry for those struggling with sexual, emotional, and relational brokenness. Finally, I truly experienced the power of Jesus' love and forgiveness at the foot of the cross.

At church, I learned to trust again, to love and receive love, and to embrace my identity as a woman in Christ alone. I learned about godly relationships between a husband and wife and saw the image of God in the marriages of fellow believers. God gave me a healthy and pure desire to date men again. In God's time and provision, a man in the support group who was also experiencing the deep love, forgiveness, and healing of Jesus Christ in his life began courting me. A year later, we were married. At the time of this writing, we are continuing to grow together after enjoying five years of a beautiful marriage that exists to glorify God and give glory to the name of Jesus. We are praying and seeking God's direction about the possibility of being parents.

In God's amazing grace and sovereignty, he has given us the passion and provided the opportunity to minister to those who struggle with various sexual sins, not just homosexuality. We seek to teach others to desire sexual purity and to follow God's design for sex exclusively between a man and a woman inside the boundaries of marriage.

As I continue in my journey of sanctification, I focus on seeking first the kingdom of God, growing in knowledge of God through his Word, letting his Word renew my mind, and being transparent through accountability and fellowship with other believers in Christ.

Not only has my life been reclaimed and restored for Christ, but my mother also came to faith in Jesus Christ, opening the door for the Lord to heal us and develop the healthy mother/daughter relationship for which I had longed. With the strength found in Christ, I have learned to forgive my parents and, with his help, am now able to have a healthier relationship with them. Now I only bring up my past to give hope to others who may have similar experiences and struggles.

(Authors' full names withheld, personal communication, June 29, 2013)

The persons described above are only a minuscule sampling of all those who have experienced God's healing and transforming power as they have submitted their lives to Christ. Many thousands of others could add their voices to give praise to God for the reality of the change he has made possible for them. When I was leading the parents' support group in Fort Lauderdale, I received monthly newsletters from a number of ministries devoted to helping those struggling with same-sex attractions. Several of these ministries regularly featured testimonies of men and women who had found freedom from homosexuality. Their words were a living witness to me of the possibility and reality of change for the struggling homosexual—and hopefully for my son.

The Bible Confirms the Possibility and Reality of Change

Although God's Word clearly condemns and prohibits homosexual practices as sinful, it just as clearly proclaims the availability of God's amazing grace, love, and forgiveness that he longs to abundantly bestow on anyone who humbly comes to him, acknowledging his or her sinful state and need of a Savior. This is the basic and critical need of all mankind, not just the homosexual, because we all stand guilty as sinners before a holy God. We all need his forgiveness.

God created us to know him and be in relationship with him, and he loved us enough to give his Son, Jesus, to die on the cross. Not only did Jesus suffer the horrendous physical pain of crucifixion, the Bible tells us he also became sin for us, taking all the sins of mankind on himself, thereby enduring God's holy and just wrath for those sins. God raised Jesus from the dead to proclaim his victory over sin and the grave and thereby opened the way to provide forgiveness of sin and to bring man into a living relationship with himself. David Platt, in his book *Radical,* sums it up this way:

> At the Cross, Christ drank the full cup of the wrath of God, and when he had downed the last drop, he turned the cup over and cried out, "It is finished." This is the gospel. The just and loving Creator of the universe has looked upon hopelessly sinful people and sent his Son, God in the flesh, to bear his wrath against sin on the cross and to show his power over sin in the Resurrection so that all who trust in him will be reconciled to God forever.[9]

We all must come the same way to God: believe the truth of God's Word, acknowledge our sin and our own helplessness to save ourselves and therefore our need of a Savior, trust in Christ's redeeming death and resurrection, and receive Jesus Christ as our personal Savior.

> Because if you confess with your mouth that Jesus is Lord and believe in your heart that God raised him from the dead, you will be saved. For with the heart one believes and is justified [made right with God] and with the mouth one confesses and is saved. (Romans 10:9-10)

The result, according to 2 Corinthians 5:17, is a brand new creation. "Therefore, if anyone is in Christ, he is a new creation. The old has passed away; behold, the new has come."

An essential part of the "new" that comes is the life of Jesus Christ that God imparts to all who accept Christ as Savior to empower them by his grace to live a changed life:

> As believers, we have access to a strength beyond ourselves that makes what seems impossible possible. God's grace is His empowering presence which enables us to be all that we were created to be and to do all that we were created to do. No one has the ability to make lasting change without the grace that a life in Christ supplies.[10]

The Bible specifically gives hope for change to those who have been involved in homosexual behavior. The most dramatic and clear statement of this truth is presented in 1 Corinthians 6:9-11. In his letter to the church at Corinth, the apostle Paul was reminding believers that "the unrighteous will not inherit the kingdom of God," and he then lists many forms of unrighteous behavior that would prevent a person from inheriting the kingdom of God, including "men who practice homosexuality."

> Do you not know that the unrighteous will not inherit the kingdom of God? Do not be deceived: Neither the sexually immoral, nor idolaters, nor adulterers, nor *men who practice homosexuality*, nor thieves nor the greedy, nor drunkards, nor revilers, nor swindlers will inherit the kingdom of God. (ESV, emphasis added)

But then Paul suddenly makes a powerful statement in verse eleven. "And such *were* some of you. But you were washed, you were sanctified, you were justified in the name of the Lord Jesus Christ and by the Spirit of our God" (ESV, emphasis added).

His meaning is clear. Former homosexuals were a part of the group of believers in Corinth, but they had experienced a deep and powerful change. They were now in a relationship with Jesus Christ, their sins forgiven and lives changed (sanctified), and the inference is that Paul personally knew these people and had witnessed the turnaround of their lives.

The necessity for this spiritual change in a person cannot be overemphasized. The most important need for the homosexual, gay or lesbian, is not to change their homosexual behavior, attractions, and urges; their deepest need, if they have never made that decision, is to come into a personal relationship with Jesus Christ. Of what eternal value would it be for a person to come out of homosexuality and even change his orientation only to be eternally separated from God because he had not trusted Christ as his Savior?

The opportunity came one night when Dan and I were talking for me to express my anxiety about this. "Dan, as concerned as I am about your homosexuality, I am more concerned about your relationship with the Lord. Where are you in your relationship to him?"

His honest response was "I don't know where I am with the Lord. I don't know what I believe any more. I've got so many questions about the Bible." But he did not encourage further discussion at that time.

And Now . . . The Rest of the Story

My friendship with John Michael, Dan's former partner, grew and deepened as our dinner meetings and conversations continued for months and then into several years. One night, John Michael was excited to inform me that he had started attending a church for the Sunday morning worship service. He liked the pastor very much and was even requesting tapes of sermons that were of particular interest to him so he could listen to them again. When he told me the name of the church, *I* got excited because it was a conservative, Bible-teaching church where I knew John Michael would clearly hear God's Word and could continue to grow in his understanding of spiritual truths.

One evening, at one of our dinner meetings, I asked John Michael directly if he knew Jesus Christ as his personal Savior, and to my relief and joy, John Michael assured me that if he died that night, he knew he would go to heaven because he believed Jesus had died for his sins so that he could. At the same time, he confessed he still had much to learn about growing in a personal relationship with Christ. That year at Christmas, he could not hold back the tears when I presented him a Bible with his name engraved in gold on the front cover.

After living in south Florida for more than thirty-eight years, I made the difficult decision to move back to Missouri, my native state, because of my elderly mother's increasing needs due to Alzheimer's. Both John Michael and I were saddened at the prospect of our separation but were determined that the many miles separating us would not obstruct our friendship. By this time, John Michael was calling me his "spiritual mom" and thanking me for helping him grow in his faith. We vowed to keep in touch, and we did. I continued to mentor him by e-mail, sending him books to read, making occasional phone calls, and suggesting Scripture verses for him to read, which he faithfully looked up in the Bible I had given him.

A couple of years after I moved to Missouri, John Michael moved back home to Ohio and, after a short time, moved in with his mother. He immediately sought out a church to attend and sent me literature from the church for my examination. This church, too, was a sound, biblically based church, and I was encouraged to read that the church had a support ministry for those struggling with homosexuality. John Michael also informed me that he had contacted one of the ministers on staff who had agreed to meet with him on a regular basis. I knew he was assuring me that he had sought help for his same-sex attractions and was even making himself accountable to one of the ministers.

In the summer of 2008, the Lord, in his foreknowledge and sovereignty, made it possible for me, while making a trip to West Virginia, to take a detour north into Ohio and spend a night with John Michael and his mother. After his mother had retired to her room, John Michael and I had a sweet time of fellowship together, talking, reading God's Word, and praying together. John Michael had been diagnosed with colon cancer in February of that year and had just completed a very intense chemo and radiation treatment program. But the prognosis was good, and the doctors were optimistic they had gotten all the cancer.

After we were alone, John Michael confessed to me that although the doctors were giving him an encouraging prognosis for the future, he still struggled with concerns and fear that the cancer would return, and this was raising questions in his mind about death. I opened my Bible and shared with John Michael assuring truths from God's Word; for Christians, death is an immediate release into the presence of God. Second Corinthians 5:8 assures those who have trusted in Christ that when they are "away from the body," they are "at home with the Lord." Because of the death of Christ and his resurrection, Christians no longer have to fear death; death has been swallowed up in victory, and lost its sting! (1 Corinthians 15:54-55) These truths from God's Word gave John Michael comfort and peace.

Amazingly, during the extremely difficult period of the cancer diagnosis and prolonged treatment, John Michael's faith had grown even stronger, and when the hospital staff questioned how he was staying so strong emotionally, he would quickly respond, "It's my faith in God and the people who are praying for me."

But the following summer, in August 2009, I was stunned to learn that John Michael had lost his courageous battle with cancer and, at the age of forty-one, had gone to his heavenly home to meet face-to-face the Savior he had come to know and follow. The news of his death hit me hard; I had come to love my "spiritual son" dearly. As I sat weeping and heartbroken, the Lord comforted me with the assurance that John Michael had trusted Christ as his Savior and now was home. Then my heavenly Father gently impressed upon my spirit this piercing and sobering question: *What if you had not been obedient when I told you to love Dan's partners?*

What *if* I had not been obedient? Would John Michael have come to know Christ? Would his life have been changed? My tears of sorrow became tears of gratitude to the Lord for opening my heart to reach out in love to John Michael so many years earlier when he was my son's homosexual partner and for giving me the grace to do it. I was strongly reminded that the reward of obedience to the Lord can be enormous—and have eternal significance.

Chapter 14

Holding On to Hope

"My soul is in anguish. How long, O LORD, how long?" (Psalm 6:3) If you are a parent, family member, or close friend of a loved one who is gay-identified or in a homosexual relationship, this may well be the recurring cry of your heart. This is especially true if you have prayed, recruited friends to pray, claimed God's promises, and believed that God would quickly answer your prayers to bring your loved one out of homosexuality and into healing of his inner struggles and same-sex attractions.

But days, weeks, months, and maybe even years have passed . . . and your hopes have not been realized. You may not see any outward signs of your loved one turning away from homosexuality, and you may begin to wonder, *Does God hear my prayers? Does he care?* When we read the psalms, we see these same struggles and honest questions expressed in the prayers of distress lifted up to God by David and other writers:

> Give ear to my words, O LORD, consider my groaning. (Psalm 5:1 ESV)

> How long, O LORD? Will you forget me forever? How long will you hide your face from me? How long must I take counsel in my soul and have sorrow in my heart all the day? (Psalm 13:1-2 ESV)

And like David, you may have wept many tears over your loved one, especially in those first days and weeks after you learned of your loved one's new identity. "I am weary with my moaning; every night I flood my bed with tears; I drench my couch with my weeping" (Psalm 6:6).

Maybe like me you have often turned to the psalms for comfort because you can so readily identify with the honest expressions recorded by those who were walking through painful and troubling times. David knew what it was to grieve the loss of a child—first, a stillborn baby and then later the death of his prodigal, rebellious, estranged but dearly loved adult son Absalom. But in Psalm 56:8, David takes comfort in the knowledge that God is very aware of all his tears: "You have kept count of my tossings; put them in your bottle. Are they not in your book?" (ESV) At one particularly painful time in my life, I was reading this verse and commented to the Lord, "Father, I think by this time I have shed so many tears you have had to exchange my bottle for gallon jugs and are running out of shelf space."

But this verse also reminds me how precious my tears are to my Father. This verse assures me that he is very aware of my "tossings;" some translations say "my laments," which means to express sorrow, mourning, or crying out in grief. Putting our tears in his bottle and recording them in his book is a beautiful metaphor of our loving Father. He collects them or makes a record of them; he does not forget the pain of our hearts. I take much comfort in that.

As time passes, the tears come less frequently and with less intensity, but the pain and longing remains. "How long, O LORD, how long?" So what do we do now? What do we hang on to? *We hold on to hope!*

At the time of this writing, it has been over twenty-one years since that unforgettable Easter Sunday afternoon, and my son still identifies himself as gay and continues in a seventeen-year, monogamous, same-sex relationship. But God continues to give me *hope*. There are times of discouragement, times when I cry out, "How long, O Lord, how long?" but always, by his Spirit and through his Word, he gives me encouragement to hold on to hope.

When I use the word *hope*, I am using the biblical definition of hope—a confident expectancy of what God is going to do. Hope does not arise from an individual's desires or wishes but from God, who is himself the believer's hope. "And now, O LORD, for what do I wait? My hope is in you" (Psalm 39:7 ESV).

Genuine hope is not wishful thinking but a firm assurance about things that are unseen and still in the future. It is a confident expectation of God's faithfulness and power to bring to pass his purposes and plans. Romans 8:24b-25 describe true hope: "Now hope that is seen is not hope. For who hopes for what he sees? But if we hope for what we do not see, we wait for it with patience" (ESV).

This verse introduces two words crucial to our holding onto hope—*wait* and *patience*—and other Scriptures confirm the importance of understanding the process of waiting with patience or endurance for the Lord to bring to pass what he has purposed. "Wait for the LORD. Be strong, take heart and wait for the LORD (Psalm 27:14), and "Be still before the LORD, and wait patiently for him" (Psalm 37:7a ESV).

But in the meantime, what can we do to help us hold on to hope?

Understand the Importance of God's Word

From the very start of this journey, God has used his Word to give me comfort, healing, wisdom, direction, and hope. When I become discouraged, his Word is a source of encouragement. The Word always points me back to God as my source of hope, and God's character gives me a solid basis for maintaining hope. His Word assures me that:

- God can do *all* things and his purposes cannot be thwarted (Job 42:1-2).
- What he has purposed he will and can do (Isaiah 46:10-11).
- He longs [waits] to show graciousness and mercy to us (*and to our children*).

The LORD longs to be gracious to you; he rises to show you compassion. Blessed are all who wait for him. (Isaiah 30:18)

He is patient, not wanting any to perish, rather desiring all to come to repentance. (2 Peter 3:9)

His Word gives me examples of real live people and how they waited patiently for God to fulfill his promises.

David was just a young shepherd boy when he was anointed by the prophet Samuel to be the next king of Israel, but he waited years before ascending to the throne. Those years of waiting were filled with many difficulties, including attempts against his life. At times, it must have seemed very unlikely that he would become king, but God's purposes for David were carried out fully and gloriously—in God's time.

Abraham was called by God to leave an idol-worshipping country, take his wife Sarah and nephew Lot, and go to an unidentified land that God promised to show him. At the same time, God gave Abraham, who was seventy-five years old and childless, a promise: "I will make of you a great nation and I will bless you and make your name great so that you will be a blessing" (Genesis 12:2). The Bible simply records, "And Abram went, as the LORD had told him . . ." (Genesis 12:4).

Abraham's belief in God's promise was demonstrated in obedience. Almost twenty-five years passed without any sign that his promise of fathering a great nation would be fulfilled. His wife Sarah remained childless. During this long, empty interval of time, when Abraham understandably became discouraged, God reiterated his promise to him, "Your offspring shall be as numerous as the stars in the sky" (Genesis 15:5). Time passed until it was physically impossible for Sarah to have a child. The Bible states plainly, "Sarah was past the age of childbearing" (Genesis18:11).

But notice carefully what the apostle Paul, under the inspiration of the Holy Spirit, wrote about Abraham in Romans 4:18-21,

Against all hope, Abraham in hope believed and so became the father of many nations, just as it had been said to him, "So shall your offspring be." *Without weakening in his faith, he faced the fact that his body was as good as dead—* since he was about a hundred years old—and that Sarah's womb was also dead. *Yet he did not waver through unbelief regarding the promise of God, but was strengthened in his faith and gave glory to God, being fully persuaded that God had power to do what he had promised.* (Emphases added)

Hang on tight to this verse. It contains much of the secret of holding on to hope!

Note the demonstration and fruit of Abraham's faith:

- Against all hope, against all the odds of having any hope, Abraham continued to hope and believe that what God had promised, he could and would bring to pass.
- Abraham did not deny the reality of his situation. He faced the facts that his body was "as good as dead," past the point where it would normally produce the necessary sperm to create a child, and Sarah's womb was also "dead"—estrogen and chromosome-bearing eggs were no longer being produced. But this "reality" did not destroy or even weaken his faith.
- Abraham is commended in Romans 4 and in Hebrews 11 for being a man of faith. He believed what God had promised. Hope is the fruit of biblical faith.
- He did not allow himself to move into unbelief concerning God's promises to him but remained "fully persuaded" that God had "power" to do what he had promised!

These power-packed verses give us great reason to hang on to hope in our situations as we continue to pray and wait on God to work in the heart and life of our loved one. Abraham knew that God could not lie; therefore, he continued believing in the face of what appeared to be overwhelming odds that God's promises would not be fulfilled. The character of God was a greater reality to Abraham than the facts that stared him in the face each day. God would be faithful, God would keep his promise, and God's purposes would not be thwarted.

Romans 15:4 underlines the value of our taking these examples from his Word for encouraging our faith and strengthening our hope: "For everything that was written *in the past* was written to teach *us*, so that through endurance and the encouragement of the Scriptures, we might have *hope*" (emphasis added). Included in the definition of endurance is the attribute of patience. Remember that word from the earlier Scripture verse in the book of Romans? "We wait for it *(hope)* patiently . . ." (Romans 8:25, emphasis added).

Realistically, there will be days when we become discouraged and it is difficult to continue holding on to hope, but thankfully, we are not left on our own to try to "work up" encouragement and hope. We are assured that God, in the persons of Father and Son, is the source of hope and encouragement and will provide the strength we need.

> May our Lord Jesus Christ himself and God our Father, who loved us and by his grace gave us eternal encouragement and good hope, encourage your hearts and strengthen you in every good deed and word. (2 Thessalonians 2:16-17)

Another strong illustration of faith and hope is shown in the account of the father of the prodigal son. When Jesus told the parable of the prodigal son in Luke 15, he gave a dramatic example of undying hope in the attitude and actions of the father toward his son. When the younger son selfishly asked his father to give him his inheritance prematurely, the father agreed. When the son then left home a few days later, taking all his possessions with him, the father let him go; he did not go after him or beg him to stay, even though he may have strongly suspected his young son would squander his inheritance. The son not only did so, he foolishly wasted it in wild and reckless living. (His older brother later alleged that the younger brother had "devoured" it on prostitutes.)

Then the account in Luke 15 tells us when the son had spent everything, a severe famine hit the land, and he was forced to take a job feeding pigs, a job far below the dignity of a young Jewish man, as pigs were considered unclean animals by Jewish law. Finally, when the son had sunk to a place of deep physical need, he came to his senses and humbly went back to his father. He went home ready to acknowledge his sinful and wrong actions and willing to take the place of a servant in his father's house.

The high point in the parable is the reaction of the father to his wayward son. We are told that while the son was still a long way off, the father saw him, felt compassion, and *ran* to embrace and kiss him. What a beautiful, emotionally charged scene! The son barely finished his rehearsed but sincere confession before the father announced a welcome home celebration for his son. He was given a royal welcome, all was forgiven, and the father rejoiced in the return of his son.

Note several things about the father:

- He relinquished control of his son, let him go, and allowed him to reap the consequences of his wrong decisions.
- He never quit loving his son and remained watchful in the hope that his son would return. While the son was still a long way off on his way home, the father saw him—evidence that each day he was waiting with patience and hope that his son would "come to his senses" and return home. The father never gave up hope.
- He welcomed his son back—not with a scolding, not with words of condemnation for his sinfulness, not with a consignment to the servants' quarters, but with compassion, love, a strong embrace, and even a kiss! Can you imagine the condition of the returning son? The dirty, stinking clothes from working with the pigs, worn out and filthy shoes—maybe no shoes at all!—and any rings he had worn when he left were gone, probably hocked for food. The father's reaction was to clothe

him with his best robe and then put a ring on his finger and shoes on his feet.

- He was not ashamed of his wayward son but threw a big celebration party, inviting everyone to rejoice with him. His son was now safely home!

This parable brings tears to my eyes. I want to be like that father, a mother who never gives up hope that her son, who has wandered afar, will return home. I am well aware that my son has not been physically or emotionally estranged from me; there has not been a break in our relationship or contact with one another, and I am eternally grateful to my heavenly Father for that. But Dan is estranged from *his* heavenly Father and is estranged from the man God created him to be. So I, too, watch and wait, with arms open wide to receive him with words of love, compassion, and rejoicing.

Some who are reading this book may be experiencing the heartache of estrangement or physical separation from your child. Your child may even be engaged in wild and reckless living like the prodigal son in this parable. Whatever your situation, I urge you to take courage and gather hope from the parable of the prodigal son and his watching, loving father, and to wait in patience, never giving up hope for what God can do in your loved one's heart and life. Pray earnestly that he, too, will someday "come home."

Scriptural Guidelines for Relating to a Prodigal

The apostle Paul, in writing to his spiritual son Timothy, gave some very wise counsel in how the Lord's servant was to respond to those who opposed him. I believe the counsel also applies aptly to how we should respond and relate to a loved one involved in homosexuality:

> The Lord's servant must not be quarrelsome, but kind to every one, able to teach, patiently enduring evil, correcting

his opponents with gentleness. God may perhaps grant them repentance leading to a knowledge of the truth, and they may come to their senses and escape from the snare of the devil, after being captured by him to do his will. (2 Timothy 2:24-26 ESV)

Note these clear guidelines for our role in the relationship:

- Do not be quarrelsome
- Be kind to everyone
- Patiently endure evil
- Correct opponents with gentleness

Then note God's part:

- He may perhaps grant them repentance.
- He may lead them to a knowledge of the truth.

We may pray for this, but it is a work of God in their hearts, which only God can do. And we should fervently pray for our sons and daughters to respond in a positive way to the Father's work in their spirits and minds so that they, like the prodigal son, will "come to their senses." This is the responsibility and decision of our loved one. We cannot make this decision for them.

Luke records that, after "coming to his senses," the prodigal son said, "I will arise and go to my father." The decision to change was followed by a definite action in the right direction. That is God's fervent desire for them, and when they make this decision, he then provides a way of escape for them. He sets them free from the snare of the Devil, their enemy, who had captured them to do his will.

These words of Paul, inspired by God's Spirit, offer not only guidelines but also hope!

IF I TELL YOU I'M GAY, WILL YOU STILL LOVE ME?

What to Do While Waiting in Hope

1. Spend time in God's Word.

Choose to believe and live by the truths of God's Word. Regular reading and meditating on God's Word will keep you focused on God's truths and enable you to discern the lies of Satan, who tries to malign the character of God and cause you to doubt him and his promises. Discouragement is a major tool of the Enemy against God's people, but God's Word is your source of encouragement.

Let me share something I have personally found helpful. When I'm reading God's Word and come across a verse that is especially meaningful, one that God is using to give me hope, assurance, or a way to pray for my son, I write Dan's name and the date by that verse in the margin in my Bible. That verse can then become a prayer I offer up to God as well as a highlighted verse for future reference. "I wait for the LORD, my soul waits, and in his Word I hope" (Psalm 130:5 ESV).

2. Pray for your child.

Do not underestimate the power of prayer. "The prayer of a righteous man is powerful and effective" (James 5:16b). As a mom seeking to be a faithful follower of Jesus Christ, I believe I can confidently read that verse this way: "The prayer of a righteous *mother* is powerful and effective."

Pray for your son or daughter that God will, by the power of his Spirit, do a strong and deep work in his or her life, drawing him or her to himself and destroying the strongholds of the Enemy in his or her mind and heart.

Again, the Scriptures give us direction on how to pray. First of all, God's Word reminds us that we are waging a spiritual battle and therefore must use spiritual weapons. Prayer is a powerful spiritual weapon that God provides us.

For though we live in the world, we do not wage war as the world does. The weapons we fight with are not the weapons of the world. On the contrary, they have divine power to demolish strongholds. We demolish arguments and every pretension that sets itself up against the knowledge of God, and we take captive every thought to make it obedient to Christ. (2 Corinthians 10:4-5)

Second Corinthians 4:3-4 also gives us some very important information that helps us to know how to pray for loved ones who are not following the Lord:

And even if our gospel is veiled, it is veiled to those who are perishing. The god of this age has blinded the minds of unbelievers, so that they cannot see the light of the gospel of the glory of Christ, who is the image of God.

We can pray that God will remove the veil from their minds, shatter the blindness that Satan has inflicted on their spiritual eyes, and expose the deception of Satan in their thinking. We can get further direction for our prayers from verse six:

For God, who said, "Let light shine out of darkness," made his light shine in our hearts to give us the light of the knowledge of the glory of God in the face of Christ.

We can pray this Scripture back to God as a prayer. "Father, just as you called the light to shine forth out of the darkness at creation, make your light shine in the heart of (name of loved one) to give (him/her) the light of the knowledge of the glory of God in the face of Christ."

Jesus made some amazing promises in regard to our prayers of faith. In Matthew 21:18-22, the account is recorded of Jesus condemning a fig tree because it bore only leaves at a time when it should have been bearing fruit. The disciples were amazed when the fig tree withered and died. Jesus used the astonishing episode of the withered fig tree to challenge the disciples to step up in their praying to a higher level of faith:

> I tell you the truth, if you have faith and do not doubt, not only can you do what was done to the fig tree, but also you can say to this mountain, "Go, throw yourself into the sea," and it will be done. If you believe, you will receive whatever you ask in prayer.

To be honest, I struggled some with what this verse meant. What did Jesus really claim was possible through prayer? I was pretty sure he wasn't giving his followers permission to go around cursing and withering fig trees or throwing mountains into the sea. But I did want to believe that somehow that account contained a promise I could claim regarding my prayers for my son.

Now I'm not a theologian, but after mediating on these verses and asking the Lord for wisdom, I believe we can confidently take away these truths from the words of Jesus:

- Jesus wants us to pray with faith and confidence in his power to do what seems impossible to the human eye and mind. In Mark 10:27, Jesus makes this statement, "With man this is impossible, but with God, all things are possible."
- God wants us to seek his face, to trust him to do great things that will bring him glory. God wants us to believe his Word, trust his promises, and ask in faith, believing he hears and will answer our prayers.

Another promise and encouragement to pray with confidence is found in 1 John 5:14-15:

> This is the confidence we have in approaching God: that if we ask anything according to his will, he hears us. And

if we know that he hears us—whatever we ask—we know
that we have what we asked of him.

The qualifier in these verses is that we ask according to his will. And
there are things we can confidently ask, knowing they *are* according
to his will—the salvation of our children, the reclaiming of who God
created them to be, and the healing work he desires to do in them.
And we can pray boldly, knowing he shares our longing in that regard.

However, the timeframe for answers to our fervent prayers has
to be left in God's hands and perfect wisdom. God must work by
his Spirit to draw people to himself, to turn their hearts toward
him, remove the Satan-inflicted blindness from their eyes, expose
the deception of the Enemy, and open their eyes to truth. He will
engineer circumstances in their lives to accomplish these purposes,
and only he knows what that means in the life of each person.

Like the prodigal son, some must sink to the level of the pigpen
before their hearts will be open to their need of him, and we must love
them enough to let them wallow there. We must trust God enough
to believe he knows best what methods to use in each life to turn a
heart toward him.

Paul Billheimer, in his book *Destined for the Throne*, writes,
"When the archives of Heaven are thrown open for the universe to
behold, it will be revealed that history was made, not in the councils
of the great, not by armies and navies, not by parliaments of nations,
but in the secluded prayer closets of the saints."

3. Pray for yourself.

As you pray for change in your loved one's life, be aware that God
may desire to make changes in your life. Honest self-examination
is needed. Am I living the kind of life and developing the kind of
relationship with the Lord that I want my child to have? Is there any
hidden sin in my own life that can hinder my prayers and perhaps
be a stumbling block to the son or daughter I am seeking to reach?

Jesus said that we first need to take the log out of our own eye before removing the speck from our brother's eye. We don't have to be afraid to admit our faults and failures to our loved ones. Humbly admitting our own sins and desire for God to change us may build a crucial bridge of communication with our loved one.

Let the Lord search your heart. Pray as King David did. "Search me, O God, and know my heart; test me and know my anxious thoughts. See if there is any offensive way in me" (Psalm 139:23-24a).

Another good prayer to pray for yourself is Psalm 19:12-14:

> Who can discern his errors? Forgive my hidden faults. Keep your servant also from willful sins; may they not rule over me. Then will I be blameless, innocent of great transgression. May the words of my mouth and the meditation of my heart be pleasing in your sight, O LORD, my Rock and my Redeemer.

An important reminder: *Guard your heart against bitterness.* God has promised that his grace is available to protect our hearts from bitterness. "See to it that no one fails to obtain the grace of God; that no root of bitterness springs up and causes trouble, and by it many become defiled" (Hebrews 12:15 ESV).

A root of bitterness growing in our hearts not only causes trouble for us but our bitter spirit will also contaminate others (family members, our loved one) around us. God's abundant grace is available; don't fail to reach out and secure it.

Your daily need for God's strength, wisdom, discernment, endurance, grace, and mercy does not diminish with the passing of time. You need to depend on your all-sufficient Father for these qualities. God can use these days of being in his waiting room to mature your faith and trust in him, to increase your knowledge of his Word, and give you a deeper understanding of his ways. This time of waiting can be a time of developing a Moses-like relationship with

God, "face to face, as a man speaks with his friend" (Exodus 33:11), or an Abraham-like faith in God, "not wavering through unbelief regarding the promises of God but . . . strengthened in his faith" (Romans 4:20). These "waiting in hope" days can be days of discovery, unearthing the treasures of darkness and gifts of riches stored in secret places (Isaiah 45:3), the treasure and gift of truly knowing Jesus Christ in a deeper, more intimate way. By God's enabling, these days will not be wasted time but time well spent for your good. We are reminded in Psalm 119:68a that God is good and does good (ESV).

4. Keep the lines of communication open.

Having open lines of communication is often the fruit of responding in love to your child. God's Word reminds us that love is not just expressed in words but also in our actions. "Dear children, let us not love with words or tongue but with actions and in truth" (1 John 3:18).

As expressed earlier in this book, we need to ask God to teach us how to show his kind of love to our loved one. First Corinthians 13 gives a detailed description of what God's kind of love looks like.

> Love is patient, love is kind. It does not envy, it does not boast, it is not proud. It is not rude, it is not self-seeking, it is not easily angered, *it keeps no record of wrongs.* Love does not delight in evil but rejoices with the truth. It always protects, always trusts, *always hopes,* always perseveres. Love never fails. (Emphases added)

This kind of love is obviously God's kind of love, not natural human love. If we try to live out this love in our own strength, we will fall far short of this standard. But when we are willing to die to our own self and seek God to fill us with his love and enabling power, it is increasingly possible to demonstrate this kind of love to others, even when they are not very lovable. "Now to him who is able to do immeasurably more than all we ask or imagine, according to his power that is at work within us . . ." (Ephesians 3:20).

Remember, we are only responsible for our own responses, attitudes, and actions. We cannot dictate or control the responses, attitudes, or actions of our loved ones. The relationship and paths of communication may be damaged or broken by their own choosing, and they may not respond in kind to our overtures of love. That is painful for the parent, family, or friend reaching out to them. But we should not allow their negative or unloving response toward us dictate our behavior. We are to be a demonstration of God's love to them as God loved us and demonstrated his love for us when we were still ungodly and alienated from him.

5. Continue to love your child and "Keep the porch light on."

Peter Lord, in his book, *Keeping the Doors Open,* urges parents to adopt an open-door policy; figuratively speaking, "Keep the porch light on." Let your loved one know that he or she can always come home or visit as often he or she wants. You may disapprove of his or her lifestyle and the choices he or she is making, but still love them and do not reject them. Don't let the separation be on your part. It's heartbreaking for the family when a son or daughter chooses to close the door of communication and walk away, cutting off all contact, perhaps even disowning the family and leaving no way for the family to maintain contact. But parents still can pray and must pray. God knows where your child is.[1]

One of the Hebrew names for God in the Old Testament is El Roi, the God who sees. It was the name by which God identified himself to Hagar, the handmaiden of Sarah, wife of Abraham, when she fled to the desert after being driven away by Sarah. When Hagar, pregnant with Abraham's child, was alone in the desert, frightened and fearful for her future, God appeared to her. He saw her; he knew her pitiful condition. Your loved one may hide from his or her family, but he or she cannot hide from God. God knows where he or she is every single moment.

6. Don't travel alone on this journey.

Reach out to others who can pray with you and sometimes just listen to you. Look for friends or family members who view life from a biblical perspective, who will stand with you in a loving and committed biblical position and provide spiritual and emotional encouragement. They also need to be compassionate, understanding, and trustworthy. At first, it is not easy to open up to others and share the deep emotional pain of having a child who is gay-identified or engaging in homosexual behavior, but carrying in isolation the burden of a loved one who is struggling with or in bondage to homosexuality is, in the long run, much more difficult and painful. You need to be able to talk with someone you can trust who, even if they don't fully understand the issues of homosexuality, will support you and love your child along with you. You need support from others in the church on this journey. Build yourself a support team, and allow God to minister to you through his church.

7. Never give up. Keep on praying.

Jesus told his disciples a parable to encourage them to keep on praying, even if they didn't seem to be getting any results from their prayers. He said they should not "lose heart" or "give up." I can relate to this parable, as it is about a widow who kept coming before a judge to present her case about being treated unfairly by an adversary, but the judge refused to even hear her case. The widow, however, persisted. She did not give up. In this parable, the judge is described as someone who neither feared God nor respected man. But eventually, the persistence of the widow began to bother him, so he finally decided to hear her case and give her justice so she would not beat him down with her continual coming before him.

Jesus summarized the truth he was teaching through the parable in this way. If an unrighteous judge who feared neither God nor man would finally yield to the persistent pleas of this poor widow, how much more will our loving heavenly Father—who is a God of love, mercy, and justice—respond to the cries of his children who cry to him night and day. He will do it "speedily" (Luke 18:1-8).

Just because we do not see things happening in the visible, physical lives of our loved ones does not mean our Father is not listening or responding to our prayers. "In every situation and circumstance of your life, God is always doing a thousand different things that you cannot see and you do not know."[2] Jesus told the Pharisees at one point, "My Father *is always at his work* to this very day" (John 5:17, emphasis added). We cannot see what God may be doing in the hearts and minds of our loved ones or what circumstances he may be arranging at this very moment, but one thing we can be sure of—God is always at his work. Take courage from this parable and these words of Jesus, and never give up! Keep on praying!

Holding on to the God of Hope!

Today, whatever your circumstances, you can have hope. Our hope is in the character of a faithful God, in the promises in his Word, in the power of prayers offered in faith in Jesus' name, and in the Holy Spirit who can work powerfully in the hearts and minds of our loved ones—and our hope is in the never-ending love of the heavenly Father for his prodigal sons and daughters.

Look to your faithful Father to keep your heart and mind filled with hope!

"May the God of hope fill you with *all joy* and *peace* as you *trust* in him, so that you may overflow with *hope* by the power of the Holy Spirit" (Romans 15:13, emphases added).

For Further Reading

Allender, Dan B. *The Wounded Heart*

Banks, James. *Prayers for Prodigals*

Butterfield, Rosaria. *The Secret Thoughts of an Unlikely Convert*

Chambers, Alan. *God's Grace and the Homosexual Next Door*

Chambers, Alan. *Leaving Homosexuality*

Consiglio, William. *Homosexual No More*

Dallas, Joe. *Desires in Conflict*

Dallas, Joe, and Nancy Heche. *The Complete Christian Guide to Understanding Homosexuality*

Dallas, Joe. *The Gay Gospel*

Dallas, Joe. *When Homosexuality Hits Home*

Davies, Bob, and Lori Rentzel. *Coming Out of Homosexuality*

Elliot, Elizabeth. *A Path Through Suffering*

Gagnon, Robert A.J. *The Bible and Homosexual Practice*

Hill, Wesley. *Washed and Waiting*

Johnson, Barbara. *Stick a Geranium In Your Hat and Be Happy!*

Johnson, Barbara. *Where Does a Mother Go to Resign?*

Moberly, Elizabeth R. *Homosexuality: A New Christian Ethic*

Nicolosi, Joseph. *A Parent's Guide to Preventing Homosexuality*

Riley, Mona, and Brad Sargent. *Unwanted Harvest?*

Saia, Michael. *Counseling the Homosexual*

Schmierer, Don. *An Ounce of Prevention*

Worthen, Anita, and Bob Davies. *Someone I Love is Gay*

Booklets

Carson, Jodi. *The Heart of the Matter—The Roots and Causes of Female Homosexuality*

Rentzel, Lori. *Emotional Dependency*

DVDs

Hamilton, Julie. *Homosexuality101*

Rogers, Sy. *One of the Boys*

Websites

www.harvestusa.org

www.livinghope.org

www.pfox.org

www.restoredhopenetwork.com

www.WaitingRoomMinistry.org

Notes

Chapter 1: A Shocking Disclosure

[1] Elizabeth Elliot, *A Path Through Suffering* (Ventura, Calif.: Gospel Light/ Regal Books, 1990), 73-74. Used by permission.

Chapter 4: Letting The Bible Clarify Homosexual Issues

[1] Robert A. J. Gagnon, *The Bible and Homosexual Practice* (Nashville: Abington, 2001), 38. Used by permission.

[2] Joe Dallas, *When Homosexuality Hits Home: What to Do When A Loved One Says They're Gay* (Eugene, Ore.: Harvest House, 2004), 51-52. Used by permission.

[3] Gagnon, *The Bible and Homosexual Practice*, 487-488.

[4] Ibid.

[5] Ibid., 37.

[6] Dallas, *When Homosexuality Hits Home*, 52-23.

[7] *Merriam-Webster's Collegiate® Dictionary, 11th Edition* ©2013 by Merriam-Webster, Inc. (*www.Merriam-Webster.com*) By permission.

[8] Alan Chambers and the Leadership Team at Exodus International, *God's Grace and the Homosexual Next Door: Reaching the Heart Of the Gay Men and Women in Your World* (Eugene, Ore.: Harvest House, 2006), 137-138. Used by permission.

[9] Mona Riley and Brad Sargent, *Unwanted Harvest?* (Nashville: B&H Publishers, 1995), 63. Used by permission of authors who now hold the copyright.

[10] Gagnon, *The Bible and Homosexual Practice*, 31.

[11] Bob Davies and Lori Rentzel, *Coming Out of Homosexuality: New Freedom for Men and Women* (Downers Grove, Ill.: InterVarsity Press, 1993), 21. Used by permission.

Chapter 5: Searching For Answers

1 Barbara Johnson, *Stick a Geranium in Your Hat and Be Happy!* (Nashville: Word Publishing, 1990), 169.

2 Joseph Nicolosi, *A Parent's Guide to Preventing Homosexuality* (Downers Grove, Ill.: InterVarsity Press, 2002), 106-107. Used by permission.

3 Dean Byrd, Shirley E. Cos, Jeffrey W. Robinson, "In Their Own Words: Gay Activists Speak About Science, Morality, Philosophy," *www.narth. com/docs/innate.html*, quoted in Joe Dallas, *When Homosexuality Hits Home: What to Do When a Loved One Says They're Gay* (Eugene, Ore.: Harvest House, 2004), 55-56. Used by permission.

4 Bob Unruh, "'Gay gene' claim suddenly vanishes," *WorldNetDaily: www. worldnetdaily.com* (May 15, 2009).

5 American Psychological Association, *Answers to Your Questions: For a better understanding of sexual orientation and homosexuality* (Washington, DC: American Psychological Association, 2008), 2. [Retrieved from *www.apa.org.*]

6 Jeffrey Satinover, "Reflections from Jeffrey Satinover," *NARTH Bulletin*, April 1995, 3, quoted in Joseph Nicolosi, *A Parent's Guide to Preventing Homosexuality* (Downers Grove, Ill.: InterVarsity Press, 2002), 62.

7 Ibid.

8 Elizabeth R. Moberly, *Homosexuality: A New Christian Ethic* (Cambridge CB1 2NT, England: Lutterworth Press, 1983), 2-3. Reprinted by permission.

9 William Consiglio, *Homosexual No More: Practical Strategies for Christians Overcoming Homosexuality* (Wheaton: Scripture Press, 1991), 22. Used by permission from author who now holds copyright.

10 Ibid., 20-22.

11 Joe Dallas, *Desires in Conflict* (Eugene, Ore.: Harvest House, 1991), 92. Used by permission.

Chapter 6: Some Answers Emerge

1 Joseph Nicolosi, *A Parent's Guide to Preventing Homosexuality* (Downers Grove, Ill.: InterVarsity Press, 2002), 19. Used by permission.

2 Mona Riley and Brad Sargent, *Unwanted Harvest?* (Nashville: B&H Publishers, 1995), 42. Used by permission of authors who now hold the copyright.

3 Joseph Nicolosi, *Reparative Therapy of Male Homosexuality: A New Clinical Approach* (Northvale, N.J.: Jason Aronson Inc., 1991), 94-95.

4 Bob Davies and Lori Rentzel, *Coming Out of Homosexuality: New Freedom for Men and Women* (Downers Grove, Ill.: InterVarsity Press, 1993), 45-46. Used by permission.

5 Elizabeth R. Moberly, *Homosexuality: A New Christian Ethic* (Cambridge CB1 2NT, England: Lutterworth Press, 1983), 15. Reprinted by permission.

6 Nicolosi, *A Parent's Guide to Preventing Homosexuality*, 31.

7 Ibid., 22.

8 Julie Hamilton, "Homosexuality 101: What Every Therapist, Parent, and Homosexual Should Know," *www.narth.com* (April 9, 2008). Used by permission.

9 Joe Dallas, *When Homosexuality Hits Home: What to Do When a Loved One Says They're Gay* (Eugene, Ore.: Harvest House, 2004), 60-61. Used by permission.

10 Julie Hamilton, *Homosexuality 101*, DVD (Orlando, Fla.: Exodus International, 2006). Used by permission.

11 Joe Dallas, *Desires in Conflict* (Eugene, Ore.: Harvest House, 1991), 94. Used by permission.

12 Dallas, *When Homosexuality Hits Home*, 61.

13 Riley and Sargent, *Unwanted Harvest?*, 50.

14 Ibid., 39.

15 Michael R. Saia, *Counseling the Homosexual* (Minneapolis: Bethany House Publications, a division of Baker Publishing Group, 1988), 55-56. Used by permission.

16 Dr. William Consiglio, *Homosexual No More: Practical Strategies for Christians Overcoming Homosexuality* (Wheaton, Ill.: Scripture Press, 1991), 37-38. Used by permission from author who now holds the copyright.

17 Ibid., 59.

Chapter 7: The Damaging Role of Sexual Abuse

1 Bob Davies and Lori Rentzel, *Coming Out of Homosexuality: New Freedom for Men and Women* (Downers Grove, Ill.: InterVarsity Press, 1993), 128. Used by permission.

2   Anita Worthen and Bob Davies, *Someone I Love Is Gay: How Family and Friends Can Respond* (Downers Grove, Ill.: InterVarsity Press, 1996), 82.

3   Davies and Rentzel, *Coming Out of Homosexuality*, 124.

4   Worthen and Davies, *Someone I Love Is Gay*, 84.

5   Don Schmierer, *An Ounce of Prevention: Preventing the Homosexual Condition in Today's Youth* (Nashville: Word Publishing, 1998), 36.

6   Joe Dallas, *When Homosexuality Hits Home: What to Do When a Loved One Says They're Gay* (Eugene, Ore.: Harvest House, 2004), 62. Used by permission.

7   Ibid., 63.

8   Davies and Rentzel, *Coming Out of Homosexuality*, 126.

9   Dallas, *When Homosexuality Hits Home*, 64.

Chapter 8: The Lesbian Factors

1   Elizabeth R. Moberly, *Homosexuality: A New Christian Ethic* (Cambridge CB1 2NT, England: Lutterworth Press, 1983), 2. Used by permission.

2   Bob Davies and Lori Rentzel, *Coming Out of Homosexuality: New Freedom for Men and Women* (Downers Grove, Ill.: InterVarsity Press, 1993), 45. Used by permission.

3   Joseph Nicolosi, *A Parent's Guide to Preventing Homosexuality* (Downers Grove, Ill: InterVarsity Press, 2002), 149. Used by permission.

4   Davies and Rentzel, *Coming Out of Homosexuality*, 45-46.

5   Don Schmierer, *An Ounce of Prevention: Preventing the Homosexual Condition in Today's Youth* (Nashville: Word Publishing, 1998), 10-11.

6   Ibid.

7   Ibid.

8   Ibid., 9-11.

9   Davies and Rentzel, *Coming Out of Homosexuality*, 53.

10 Ibid., 49.

11 Ibid., 59-60.

12 Michael R. Saia, *Counseling the Homosexual* (Minneapolis: Bethany House Publications, a division of Baker Publishing Group, 1988), 57-58. Used by permission.

13 Carol Ahrens, quoted by Joe Dallas, *Desires in Conflict* (Eugene, Ore., Harvest House, 1991), 203. Used by permission.

14 Ibid., 204.

15 Ibid., 205-206.

16 Ibid., 206-207.
17 Nicolosi, *A Parent's Guide*, 161.
18 Ibid., 164.

Chapter 9: Looking Back

1   Bob Davies and Lori Rentzel, *Coming Out of Homosexuality: New Freedom for Men and Women* (Downers Grove, Ill.: InterVarsity Press, 1993), 44-45. Used by permission.
2   Michael R. Saia, *Counseling the Homosexual* (Minneapolis: Bethany House Publications, a division of Baker Publishing Group, 1988), 50. Used by permission.
3   Joe Dallas, *When Homosexuality Hits Home, What to do When a Loved One Says They're Gay* (Eugene, Ore.: Harvest House, 2004), 71. Used by permission.
4   Ibid., 73-74.
5   Ibid., 75.

Chapter 12: Partners: A Package Deal?

1   Alan Chambers and the Leadership Team at Exodus International, *God's Grace and the Homosexual Next Door: Reaching the Heart of the Gay Men and Women in Your World* (Eugene, Ore.: Harvest House, 2006), 128. Used by permission.
2   Robert A. J. Gagnon, *The Bible and Homosexual Practice* (Nashville: Abington, 2001), 296. Used by permission.
3   Ibid., 297.
4   Peter Sprigg, *The Top Ten Myths About Homosexuality* (Washington, DC: Family Research Council, 2010), 44.
5   Ryan Lee, "Gay Couples Likely to Try Non-monogamy, Study Shows," *Washington Blade* (August 22, 2003), 18, quoted in Peter Sprigg, *The Top Ten Myths About Homosexuality* (Washington, DC: Family Research Council 2010), 45.
6   Sprigg, *The Top Ten Myths*, 46.
7   Lawrence Kurdek, "Are Gay and Lesbian Cohabitating Couple *Really* Different from Heterosexual Married Couples?" *Journal of Marriage and Family 66* (November 2004): 893, quoted in Peter Sprigg, *The Top Ten Myths About Homosexuality* (Washington, DC: Family Research Council, 2010), 46.
8   Gagnon, *The Bible and Homosexual Practice*, 452.

Chapter 13: Change: A Possibility? A Reality?

1   Peter Sprigg, *The Top Ten Myths About Homosexuality* (Washington, DC: Family Research Council, 2010), 8.

2   Edward O. Laumann, John H. Gagnon, Robert T. Michael, and Stuart Michaels, *The Social Organization of Sexuality: Sexual Practices in the United States* (Chicago: University of Chicago Press, 1994), 290-301, quoted in Peter Sprigg, *The Top Ten Myths About Homosexuality* (Washington, DC: Family Research Council 2010), 8.

3   Crystal Dixon, *Toledo Free Press,* quoted by Ron Prentice, *PFOX newsletter, ProtectMarriage.com* (August 12, 2009).

4   Robert Spitzer, M.D., "Can Some Gay Men and Lesbians Change Their Sexual Orientation? 200 Participants Reporting a Change from Homosexual to Heterosexual Orientation," *Archives of Sexual Behavior* 32, no. 5 (October 2003): 413, quoted in Peter Sprigg, *The Top Ten Myths About Homosexuality* (Washington, DC: Family Research Council, 2010), 13.

5   J. Nicolosi, A.D. Byrd, and R.W. Potts, "Retrospective self-reports of changes in homosexual orientation: A consumer survey of conversion therapy clients," *Psychological Reports* 86, pp. 689-702. Cited in: Phelan et al., p. 12, quoted in Peter Sprigg, *The Top Ten Myths About Homosexuality* (Washington, DC: Family Research Council, 2010), 11.

6   Michael Foust, "Study: Ex-gay ministry has 53 percent success rate," *Baptist Foundation Press, News from a Christian Perspective* (August 10, 2009). Used by permission.

7   See "Christine," *believe, Connecting Life & Faith, Christian Devotional Magazine* (October 2000). Used by permission.

8   Willy Torrensin, "Will You Accept My Love?" *Exodus Global Alliance: www.exodusglobalalliance.org,* (February 21, 2013).

9   David Platt, *Radical: Taking Back Your Faith From the American Dream* (Colorado Springs: Multnomah, 2010), 36.

10   Alan Chambers, *Exodus International newsletter,* vol. 5, issue 1 (January 2010).

Chapter 14: Holding On To Hope

1   Peter Lord, *Keeping the Door Open: What To Do When Your Child Wanders from God* (Grand Rapids: Chosen Books, 1992), 60.

2   John Piper, "The Ultimate Meaning of True Womanhood" (lecture, Chicago, IL, October 2008), quoted in Nancy Leigh DeMoss, *Voices of the True Woman Movement* (Chicago, Ill.: Moody Publishers, 2010), 84.

28776429R00136

Made in the USA
Lexington, KY
03 January 2014